TEACH YOUR BABY

A COMPLETE TESTED PROGRAM OF SIMPLE DAILY ACTIVITIES FOR INFANTS AND SMALL CHILDREN, DESIGNED TO DEVELOP LEARNING ABILITIES TO THE FULLEST POTENTIAL

Genevieve Painter, Ed. D.

DRAWINGS BY LORETTA TREZZO

CORNERSTONE LIBRARY

Published by Simon & Schuster
NEW YORK

To My Parents
Max and Amelia Berkowitz

Published by Cornerstone Library
A Simon & Schuster Division of
Gulf & Western Corporation
Simon & Schuster Building
1230 Avenue of the Americas
New York, New York 10020

CORNERSTONE LIBRARY and colophon are
trademarks of Simon & Schuster, registered in
the U.S. Patent and Trademark Office.

This Cornerstone Library edition is a revised
and updated edition of the original hardcover
book published by Simon & Schuster.

Manufactured in the United States of America

10 9 8 7 6 5 4 3 2 1

LIBRARY OF CONGRESS CATALOGING IN PUBLICATION DATA

Painter, Genevieve.
  Teach your baby.

  Reprint. Originally published: New York : Simon and
Schuster, 1971.
  1. Ability in children. 2. Intellect—Problems,
exercises, etc. 3. Learning, Psychology of—Problems,
exercises, etc. 4. Infant psychology. 5. Education,
Preschool. I. Title.
BF723.A25P34   1982   649'.1   81–22200
                                            AACR2

ISBN 0–346–12558–8 (pbk.)

CONTENTS

FOREWORD

IT IS REFRESHING to see a book for parents that does not merely give them the generalities found in the usual clichés—"All the child needs is enough love"; "You must have patience"; "You must not demand too much from your child"; or "You must not repress your child." Instead of these clichés, here we have a book which describes in great detail the training methods that parents can and should apply—with great benefit—to their very young children.

Parents have few guidelines offering them a distinction regarding what one should or should not do; therefore they do not have specific ideas or well-planned methods of child-rearing. Having few specific guidelines, parents usually do what seems to be best at a given moment. These actions, although well-meant, are guided by the parents' feelings of the moment and are merely expedient ways of handling a situation; they are not well-studied or planned actions for long-lasting training or learning.

To know specifically how to train young children to make the most of their abilities to learn and develop and progress throughout their childhood is more imperative now than ever before. In the past, children grew up in large families where the older took care of the younger and all accepted responsibility for household chores. Each child was exposed to the stimulation and activities of his siblings, and the mother was free to supervise the running of the household and to spend much of her time with the baby providing special stimulation.

Today the situation is different. Even though there may be fewer children in the family, many mothers find it difficult to concern themselves with the development of each baby. These mothers have not learned how to achieve cooperation from their children or how to cope with the many ways in which children demand undue attention through disturbing means, and so the mother's attention, though often constant, is nonconstructive. Because mothers feel defeated by this losing game, they are often exhausted and are only too happy to have a little rest and quiet when the children do not provoke them. Thus we find in our families that insufficient time and preparation are given for constructive activities with mutual fun and enjoyment.

Dr. Painter has made a considerable contribution to parents and children of today. She has introduced a new element in the care of the very young by outlining a way of "teaching" infants. It has been self-evident that the infant "learns" about himself and life in the process of growing up; it was, however, less clear that a mother can begin to "teach" a baby within the first weeks of his life.

The planned play activities presented in this book permit every mother to be highly effective in her interactions with her child, even though the time required in the daily schedule is relatively short. It is not the *amount* of time the mother spends with the baby but the *quality* of that time that is important and productive. Instead of her often nonconstructive attention dependent upon her impulses and feelings of the moment, the mother now has a preplanned schedule of activities, which should make it much easier for her to take the necessary time for the baby. The modern mother can now plan and maintain a routine with the same ease as the mother of past generations with a large family, who found herself obliged to plan a schedule. This book should help the mother with several children establish a natural order in the family in which it is possible for each child to relate to the others without fighting, controlling, subduing, or giving in and to grow physically, emotionally and intellectually. The mother of a single child will find the book equally helpful and rewarding.

It is our experience that parents can easily learn what to do, provided information is given to them in terms of practical steps and procedures. This, Dr. Painter does admirably. Every mother who wants to help her baby in his development can start the orderly and planned activities suggested in this book as soon as the baby is born. She will soon discover how pleasurable the activities are and how effectively they encourage and motivate the baby's desire to learn.

RUDOLF DREIKURS, M.D.
Professor Emeritus, Chicago Medical School
Founder, Community Child Guidance Centers of Chicago

INTRODUCTION

As we are fast approaching the twenty-first century, we must review the educational processes needed to prepare our children for the technological and ecological changes projected for the future. Babies born in the 1980s will become the young adults of the twenty-first century. They must be educationally prepared to develop imagination and creativity and provide whatever is needed for mankind's next step. These young adults will be the children who learn to think for themselves, use their creative abilities, and especially be able to work tenaciously to translate their ideas into reality. Your baby can become one of these important young adults, and the groundwork for these constructive abilities can begin in your very own home.

TEACH YOUR BABY gives you the tools to work with in stimulating your child from birth to three years of age. By opening many new dimensions toward his intellectual development, you can start now in preparing him for success in his future schooling.

Research in Infant Education

Educators are increasingly convinced that training a child receives during infancy from his parents is the major factor in his development of the intellectual skills and concepts that will later enable him to work effectively in school. Benjamin S. Bloom summarizes, in *Stability and Change in Human Characteristics,* the research of one thousand different studies of infant growth made over the last fifty years. These studies closely agree that the child's most active period of growth, both physically and intellectually, takes place between birth and age four, at which time his IQ becomes well established. That is, a person's IQ at four fairly accurately predicts what his IQ will be at the age of seventeen. It is in the first years of a child's life, therefore, that parents most profoundly influence their child's future intelligence, his potential to learn.

What is infant intelligence and how is it measured? A baby's IQ is indicated by his motor ability, by his physical actions and by his alertness. IQ is tested by observing the baby's actions and reactions and comparing them to the charted developmental averages of other babies of the same age. The behavior of thousands of babies has been carefully observed and recorded in order to determine the average or norm for each age level. As the child grows, of course, the tests become more complex. By observing and comparing many infant abilities, the tests reveal the basic ingredients of intelligence: sensorimotor coordination, language ability, memory, reasoning, conceptual understanding, the ability to abstract, to make associations, to follow instructions.

Causes of School Failure

By the early 1960s, educators were aware of the increasing numbers of children who were failing in school. A majority of these failing children were from very poor families. As early as age three, many children already demonstrated deficiencies in the basic skills that are essential to learning in school. These kinds of deficiencies hold back proper learning in first grade. For example, a preschool child who cannot distinguish among various shapes and forms, or see how pieces fit together to make a whole, as in a jigsaw puzzle, will have great difficulty in learning to read, which depends on recognition of far subtler differences among individual letters and words. In trying to evaluate the causes for such failure child-development experts agreed that one reason might be lack of early training from parents. Burdened and preoccupied with the serious problems of survival, parents of the lower income groups are often unable to play with their children, to talk and explain to them, and to otherwise stimulate them with toys and books. It was decided that a preschool experience might make up some of the deficits and prevent some educational problems from arising later.

And so the Head Start program, operated by the Office of Economic Opportunity and supported by Federal funds, came into being. Classes began in 1965 with 500,000 four- and five-year-olds, who were provided with six to eight weeks of preschool experience. It soon became obvious that this was not adequate, and the program was expanded to cover first one, then two full years of preschool education. There were IQ gains, but these were often lost when the children entered an ordinary first grade. Though evidently on the right track, Head Start was clearly still too late.

In order to facilitate growth at an even earlier age, Head Start programs were initiated for infants as young as six months of age. In one of these, the Parent-Child Center in Mt. Carmel, Illinois, I personally instituted the TEACH YOUR BABY program. Other Parent-Child Centers throughout the country used these activities extensively and found them to be very effective.

For educators and researchers, this Head Start experience has emphasized the great importance of the first three years of life to the development of intelligence. The role of home and family in child development has become a subject of ever-increasing interest and study.

How Parents Affect the Development of Intelligence

During the first three years of life parents are, naturally, the most important people in the child's life. His first environment, his home and family, contributes heavily toward the growth of his mind and later development. A warm relationship with mother, father, brothers and sisters develops his self-confidence. In such an environment a child feels he belongs and is valued by others; he learns to trust others. Opportunities for sensorimotor learning through seeing, hearing, feeling and moving help the baby learn about things and also about himself, his body, his abilities. His parents and older brothers and sisters are usually delighted and surprised by his progress. This important reaction to the baby encourages him to continue his efforts and to explore his world. Playing with all members of the family helps him to adapt to different people, to know his family and to respond differently to each person who plays with him. Encouraging him to amuse himself develops his independence and ability to cope with problems. Through imaginative play with ordinary objects—the water faucet, the door hooks, the screwdriver— he learns about being grown up. He distinguishes the familiar from the new. He learns about space—where things are in relationship to himself and to other things. This ideal home —warm, friendly and well disciplined—helps the child learn to learn.

In average homes, most parents act similarly during the first year. According to Burton L. White, Harvard's Preschool Project Director, it is during the baby's second year that the behavior of parents begins to differ widely from one family to another. He claims that the toddler's curiosity, his zest for learning and grasp of language, all lead the effective mother to speak to the baby and try to satisfy his now more sophisticated needs. However, to other mothers the growth of the baby only means that he may endanger himself and thus will require more attention and care from her. In large families of small dependent children, the mother is likely to concentrate on keeping the baby out of the way.

From the studies of the Harvard research team, it is obvious that the child of the mother who is able to provide a variety of experiences and who is able to play with and teach her child in a calm manner is most likely to do well both emotionally and intellectually in infancy and in nursery school, not to mention later in school. While deficiencies in mothering cut across class lines, the middle-class child, black and white, has the best chance of having a more capable mother who is more readily available to the child. Researchers also agree that most parents are unaware of the methods of enriching their baby's environment in a meaningful way. The program presented in this book trains parents to become aware of and use the means to create an environment stimulating to their baby's growing intelligence.

Background of the Program in This Book

In 1963 I became interested in the field of special education. Along with other researchers, I was alarmed at the number of children who arrived at nursery school at age three or four, at kindergarten, and at first grade unable or unwilling to learn what teachers tried to teach.

At about this time I was invited to develop and supervise an educational research program undertaken by the University of Illinois and funded by the United States Office of Education. The object of the research was to determine whether babies who were tutored for a year would show a significant IQ increase over those who had no tutoring. The research was divided into two phases.

In the first phase, two professional teachers and I began simply by playing with babies in their own homes, much as a parent might do. However, we applied psychological principles of infant development, aiming for the most effective method of teaching the things we considered necessary to the baby's success in future schooling: use of their senses; of their bodies, particularly their hands; use of language; ability to solve problems; picture comprehension, etc.

The thirty babies selected for the program were eight- to twenty-four-month-olds, healthy, and normal in IQ. They were tested and randomly assigned to two groups—those to be tutored, called the experimental group, and those not to be tutored, called the control or comparison group. At the end of a year of tutoring by professional teachers, the experimental group were found to average ten points higher in IQ than the control babies, whose IQs remained at the level of the previous year.

In the next year, the second phase of the research, parents were trained in the educational activities and child-rearing methods used by the professional teachers in the previous year. These parents then began to teach their own babies, ages five months to twenty-four months. The babies worked happily in play activities with their parents for as long as an hour at one stretch. At the end of one year, the babies who had been tutored by their own parents averaged sixteen points higher in IQ than the control babies who had received no special tutoring.

There were differences more obvious than IQ scores between both groups of experimental children and the control children. The children of the experimental groups were more alert and were able to do many more things. A teacher or a parent taught each experimental child how to use his hands and body, and stimulated his imagination, his ability to reason, to abstract and to make associations, etc. The children were encouraged to feel that they are capable of learning and of doing many things; therefore, they were willing to learn and to work, and they were also willing to perform for the test examiner—they were "motivated" to work.

The child's capacity to learn or his potential is not a fixed quantity. If his environment is active and stimulating, his capacity or potential is greatly increased.

These findings are significant to professional educators, both teachers and teachers of teachers. Of even greater interest is their importance to parents, who prove to be the most effective teachers of their own babies.

The methods used in our program by parents and teachers are presented in this book. The earliest activities, from birth to age seven months, were developed in Champaign-Urbana, Illinois and in Mt. Carmel, Illinois, with individual parents who tried them when teaching their own babies.

Kathleen A. Walton, Director/Owner of Adlerian Child Care Center and Kindergarten, Columbia, South Carolina, is a preschool teacher who has been using this book in her classrooms since it was first published ten years ago. She writes, "The strength of this book, TEACH YOUR BABY, is the systematic approach for categorizing learning experiences at different age levels with a great variety of learning activities. Teachers readily understand the objectives in the learning activities and by using this text can plan a learning program that is comprehensive, varied, and effective. Our child care program uses the activities for infants starting at six months of age. The book is complete, adaptable, and practical for a day care early learning program."

I feel privileged to have worked in this pioneer research. I am grateful to the Alfred Adler Institute of Chicago, the United States Office of Education, the University of Illinois, and the Parent-Child Center, Mr. Carmel, Illinois, and to all the people who worked with me and supported the program, especially the parents and their lively babies without whom there would be neither a program nor a book.

It is my firm belief that any parent who uses this approach and applies it regularly and consistently can stimulate the intellectual development of his baby to a point that surpasses the highest professional anticipation for school entry. I continue to enjoy sharing the ideas of this most exciting experience with parents everywhere who are asking, "What shall I teach my baby?"

CHAPTER I | # NEWBORN BABIES ARE READY TO LEARN

Babies Are Born Active

YOUR NEW BABY is "born active," capable of doing a number of things. Just think of it: a new baby can cry, sneeze, hiccough, suck his thumb, suck for milk, follow a light with his eyes, smile (some say it's gas), cling to your finger, and even raise his body as you help pull him up. These activities are called "reflexes." The baby's reflexes are capable of reacting differently at different times, depending on the situation. For example, a baby who is crying and angry is more likely to support his weight when clinging to your fingers than a baby who is well fed and peaceful. A baby may stop nursing when shown a bright light, or stop crying when he hears something.

A Baby's Senses

All of the baby's sense organs are ready to function at birth or within a few hours afterwards. Of course, this does not mean that he can understand the world as we know it. What we know about the world we have learned through long experience and maturation. There was a time when we were babies, when we looked around and did not see things as they are. We could not pick out individual objects, we could not even separate ourselves from the "out there." However, the baby at birth is equipped to start on his long journey of learning about the large area outside himself that we call his "environment." All of his learning takes places through his senses, which are ready to start teaching him. The baby's senses of seeing, hearing, feeling, tasting, smelling and moving allow him to reach out toward environment and thus to learn about it.

How Babies Are Alike

Although babies are very different, all babies are alike in some ways. Individual though he is, your infant has much in common with infants everywhere. Through heredity he receives some characteristics that are common to all humans —*uniformities*—and some that are uniquely his—*differences*. His growth takes place in an orderly sequence because human maturation of nerves, muscles and other tissues is a uniform development. Maturation has been studied in great detail by child developmentalists who have charted the "normal" or usual development of children. They can tell us, for example, that if you place a newborn baby on his stomach he will lie still (at first). In time he will begin to gain control of the muscles supporting his head and he will then be able to lift his head, at first for a moment, and then for longer periods of time. Because of the natural developmental sequence of the human race, it is certain that the healthy infant will someday sit up, creep, crawl and finally be able to assume an erect posture and walk. These *uniformities* are passed on from one generation of human beings to another through *uniformities* in genes.

How Babies Are Different

Individual *differences* are passed on to the infant in his heredity through differences in genes. No developmental chart can tell you the exact time at which your child will be sitting, crawling, walking or talking. There may be very

definite developmental differences between your child and
another, and these differences may be great among healthy,
normal children. Individual differences are further influ-
enced by the kinds of experiences the infant has.

How Babies Learn

Since the baby is capable of learning from the moment of
his birth, the kinds of stimulation his senses receive will, of
course, influence his development. For example, the infant
who is reared in an institution, with very little care other
than feeding and diaper changing, will not have the learning
experiences of the infant reared at home by loving parents
who play with him. An infant reared in an institution will
be far slower in development than the child reared at home.
Yet, in spite of all the educational experiences a parent can
offer his baby, the child is limited by nature: for example,
no baby will sit up without support at twelve weeks, but at
thirty-six to forty-four weeks, most will. We know too that
the walking baby at times will go back to creeping and the
child who has learned a dozen words may temporarily come
to a halt in his speech development, or even go back to an
earlier stage and just babble for a time. This turning back is
an important and necessary part of development. By practicing behavior of a previous stage, the child can master the
abilities that will enable him to advance to higher levels of
achievement.

TEACH HIM HOW TO BECOME A FAMILY MEMBER

All his life the child will have to adjust to the
needs of others. Relationships with other people are first
learned within the family; parents must help teach their

children how to get along and to cooperate with people. Right from the start you can allow your baby to learn that he is a member of the family. It is far better for the child to enter the family group as a sharing rather than as a receiving member. He should not be allowed needlessly to change the entire routine of living, or to feel that he is the center of interest, the reason for the family's existence. It is not a kindness to make him the hub of the universe. Parents who center their attention around the child as an infant themselves often tire of this when he gets older; and certainly the world at large will not treat him with such importance. A baby must have food, sleep and loving attention, but the less disturbance he causes in the natural routine of the family, the better.

A Feeding Schedule

The establishment of a feeding schedule, which teaches the baby to fit into family life and to cooperate, should take into consideration the infant's needs, and, of course, your pediatrician should be consulted. Pediatricians vary in their advice on feeding schedules, but all seem to agree that the baby will eventually establish a regular interval between feedings, and the establishment of a natural rhythm of feeding and other biological functions will help the baby in his physical and social development. Most of the problems in feeding result from the parent's anxiety. If the baby is on "self-demand" feeding, the overanxious parent indulges him and gives him food whenever he stirs; if he is on "four-hour" feeding, she sits and waits with increasing tension while the baby cries for that last half hour. A few minutes earlier or later in feeding make little difference; however, the parent's attitude is very important. She should be calm and quiet when she feeds the baby. Though some parents find it hard to believe, worry over feeding is totally unnecessary. Since eating is dependent upon hunger, we can rely upon hunger to take over that part of the teaching job which creates the appetite. The baby "knows" how much he should eat. If he eats more at one feeding, he might need less at the next. This part the mother does not have to teach, and this knowledge should ease the worry about quantity, once the pediatrician has been consulted. The mother's job is only to teach the scheduling and to teach it without anxiety.

Baby's Rights, Family's Rights

Cooperation, order and regularity are essential to the unity of family living. When the infant is nursed at the breast or by the bottle he is beginning to learn to cooperate with another family member. In a cooperative effort, both parties have rights and needs. In the case of nursing, the baby needs to receive nourishment and, further, needs to learn how to cooperate in getting it. The mother needs to be able to teach cooperation according to her own style and should feel free to include her own convenience in the scheduling. Thus nursing becomes a kind of model of mutuality that will exist in all the baby's future relationships. No mother does her child justice when she "sacrifices all for the good of the baby." Such an attitude creates difficulty for the child and for the family as a whole. For a happy family existence, we must be concerned with the rights and needs of parents and other children as well as the rights and needs of the baby.

To Sleep or Not to Sleep

The baby has a need to sleep and to receive love and attention. Of course you love your baby, and it is important that you express this love. Love is the most satisfying of human experiences. By giving the baby love and attention when he is awake you teach him to cooperate in family life. However, the baby must also be taught that crying for attention when he is well-fed, dry and otherwise comfortable will not bring him attention. At times, parents actually teach babies not to sleep. If the baby is well cared for and still cries, the anxious mother hovers over him, picks him up and cuddles him. As soon as he stops crying and she puts him down, he starts crying and she picks him up again. The baby soon learns that if he does not sleep, if he cries, he can make his mother appear. This baby is being taught not to sleep.

Sometimes the proud parents feel that the baby is a new toy. They awaken him so that visitors can see what a fine specimen he is. But the baby has a right to sleep, and his parents are showing a lack of respect for him by not observing *this* right. It is not, however, necessary to tiptoe and keep the house quiet while the baby sleeps. This can infringe on the rights of the other family members. The baby can easily learn to sleep while there is some action in the home.

The Best Time to Play

Giving the baby love and attention at the appropriate time is important to his well-being. Playing with children is fundamental to building a good relationship with them, and you can start by playing with your baby for a few minutes when he is awake and peaceful. Just as in other training, you should not give him attention by playing with him when he cries for no apparent good reason. That only reinforces crying for attention. The time to play is when he is in a pleasant mood. Parents do not always know how to play with young children, especially with babies. This book attempts to tell parents the kinds of things that can be done in play that teach the baby skills and at the same time teach him to get along with other people by helping him become a family member.

STRUCTURE THE BABY'S WORLD FOR MAXIMUM DEVELOPMENT

After you have washed, diapered, fed and cuddled your baby, it is time to consider how to structure the baby's world so that it has the greatest positive effect on his growth.

The Home Atmosphere

A relaxed, comfortable home atmosphere helps the baby learn. The usual family noises of laughing and talking, doing the dishes, running the vacuum cleaner are all sounds that he will learn to think of as friendly. The home should be run in an orderly manner so that each member of the family knows there is an overall schedule and that certain things happen at regular times. A regular time for meals, naps, play and bedtime is essential to the training of children. An orderly home prevents many discipline problems from arising. A home, however, in which the radio or TV are continually blaring, in which family members shout at each other and fight, and in which irregular habits of eating and sleeping prevail, is disturbing to all the family, and discipline problems are fostered.

Teach Baby Through Play

A daily family schedule should be made to help the family members live in the home with ease and should include a plan for teaching the baby. This book is designed to help you make and carry out a teaching plan which will be effective and fun for both you and the baby. The activities are grouped by order of difficulty in sections and chapters and match the growth rate of most babies. Throughout this book you will see pictures and descriptions of toys and other materials from which to choose in planning daily educational play. In order to give each baby the possibility of play activities that will be just right for his stage of development and for his particular interests and enjoyment, I have included many more activities than you will want to use. As a matter of fact, it would be confusing to the child to give him too many toys or activities. You can choose by observing the baby as you play with him and trying the different activities to see which he enjoys and does with ease, which he finds difficult and frustrating, and which he finds interesting and challenging.

HOW TO PLAN DAILY LESSONS

Your daily lesson plans should have these major types of activity:

1. *Activities all by himself before falling asleep or after awakening:* These would include observing toys and objects hung from his crib or playpen when he is very young; later they would including playing with toys he could reach by himself.

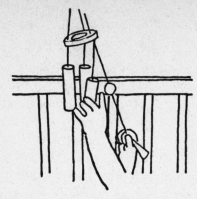

2. *Activities for informal play:* As he gets older and stays awake for longer periods of time, some toys and other objects should be planned for his use when he plays informally, by himself or with others, in his playpen, his own room or elsewhere. When he is old enough to walk, run and climb, equipment for large muscle movements should be made available to him.

3. *Activities for structured daily lessons:* Each day a special structured play period should be given to the baby. This should be a certain time set aside during the day in which you and the baby can play together without interruption. During the first few months of his life you will not be able to plan many structured lessons because it is important to allow the baby to get adequate rest. It will be necessary to fit his play into his short waking periods. Once the baby is able to stay awake for longer periods and to sit at his table, you should plan fifteen-minute to half-hour lessons, and later, one-hour lessons. For these lessons you will want to plan ahead in detail. Observe what the baby is actually able to do and then read the sections in the book for ideas on activities for his age and developmental level.

Familiar and Unfamiliar Skills

When teaching a child it is important to encourage further development of partially developed skills and also to concentrate on skills which the child does not know at all. One must therefore include activities emphasizing skills which the child is able to do with ease, as well as skills with which he is unfamiliar. For example, you will first observe your baby and decide upon some of the things he is able to do. Then look at the chapter for his age level and try to match some activities in each category of training (seeing, hearing, feeling, imitation, language, etc.) to his own levels. It is a good idea to study the chapters previous to and following the one that discusses his present age level so that you will find the activities best suited to his development.

Fitting a Plan to your Baby's Skills

A suggested plan follows:

If your baby: (1) grasps with thumb and three fingers; (2) reaches for objects; (3) gets angry and frustrated when he wants to pick up a toy and already has something in each hand; and (4) coos when you talk to him, you might plan the following activities during one week:

1. Give him rather large objects to pick up, because he does not yet have the coordination for picking up very small things. Give him some smaller objects to pick up so that he can at least try; if he gets angry, stop that activity and try again in a week or two.

2. Offer him objects out of his reach so that he practices reaching and strengthens an already developed skill.

3. While he is holding an object in each hand show him a third object. If he does not know that he must drop one in his hand to pick up the one you are offering, take one away from him as you give him the third object. Do this several times so that he will get the idea. Understanding the need for releasing an object before picking up another will train both his intellect and his coordination.

4. Start giving him activities to stimulate imitation,

which is the beginning of his language training (see Chapter VII).

5. Give him activities to stimulate his senses of seeing, hearing and feeling (see Chapter VII).

6. Help him learn cause-effect relationships (the beginning of intellectual training) by hanging a toy over his crib which makes a noise when he hits it.

Time to Repeat, Time to Explore

Little children like to do things over and over again. They should be allowed time to repeat an activity so that they may develop their attention span and be given time to explore new ways or uses of materials to stimulate the imagination. It is, of course, necessary to use common sense with your choice of activities. If the child is not yet speaking, it would be sensible to give him the imitation and pre-speech activities. It would be a poor choice to give him the language training suggested toward the end of the book. Suggested lesson plans for each age level are given at the end of each chapter to help you make plans for your own baby.

Organizing Toys and Structured Playtime

It is important that the toys you select for the structured program not be treated as ordinary toys. They should be kept separate from his other toys and taken out for use *only* during the structured playtime. They will then continue to be attractive to the baby and remain a source of excitement and stimulation for creative and intelligent activity. A cardboard carton or, better yet, a plastic laundry basket can be used as a container for the special toys that will be kept out of the child's reach until his structured playtime. You should then give him only one toy or object at a time with which to work. It would be a good idea to keep a notebook in which you plan ahead for the daily lessons. Write what you want

to review or do again, and the new thing you want to try. You should also record what he is able to do, unable to do, and what he enjoys doing.

Corner for Play Lessons

Since his first years are the most important learning years of his life, you should set aside a corner for structured play lessons even for the newborn. It should be thought of as a flexible area in which you might use a table and chair or a playpen, or remove them and use the floor. He will eventually be happy to work at his table with his parent as his teacher for an hour—he may even wish to play still longer. Although it is best to start at birth, teaching your baby can begin at any age; for the purposes of this book, at any age from infancy to two years or more.

BEYOND THE VALUE OF FUN AND PLAY

The activity programs in this book are designed for fun and play because babies and very young children learn through play. A baby's play, beyond the pleasure it gives him, teaches him how to use his eyes, ears, hands and body; more important, he develops a good relationship with the parent who plays with and teaches him.

A Baby's Perceptions—the Basis for Learning

From the moment of birth the baby's impressions of his environment are revealed to him slowly, hour by hour, day by day. Seeing, hearing, feeling, tasting and smelling things start his senses working, which then let his brain learn. These early learnings are called "perceptions" and the lessons you will give him at first are "perceptual lessons." Perception is fundamental to later learning—it is the basis of language and reading. Remember that even a young baby solves problems. He quickly learns to cry for feeding and to smile, cry, or reach out when he wants to be picked up. Your goal will be to let him learn to do many things for himself so that he later realizes that he is able to learn and to do things. He will develop good feelings about himself, about family members, and later about school. He will be "motivated" to learn—that is, he will be interested in learning and be willing to work until a task is learned. All of these lay the foundations for future learning.

TOYS AND EQUIPMENT

It is important to note that expensive toys are not necessarily better teaching tools than inexpensive toys or toys that are made at home. The success or failure of the program will depend less upon the amount and cost of equipment than upon the ingenuity and planning of the parent, the type of relationship between parent and child, and the regularity of daily lessons. In our research program we found pictures cut from magazines were excellent for making books and puzzles, and for teaching vocabulary and the classification of objects; they also taught the child creative use of available materials.

FATHERS ARE GOOD TEACHERS TOO

It is apparent to all of us that the role of the father has changed. It is wonderful for our families that fathers now share in the rearing of their children and they find increasing satisfaction in fatherhood. Playing with your child puts you in a position of truly being able to influence him because play serves to build a relationship of love, mutual respect, and trust. The wise father, like the wise mother, will spend some playtime with the baby each day.

This book is meant for either or both parents as a teacher; when I use the word *mother* or *she* it includes *father* or *he*. And, when writing about the baby, the term *he* includes *she* if your baby is a girl. Please forgive the economy of words.

HAVE FUN, BUT DO NOT TIRE BABY

Do not tire the baby. You can tell when play and learning are good for him—he will smile, coo, reach for toys and for your hand. When he is restless or fussy he probably is telling you that he is tired, hungry, or that he has had enough play. Or he may be telling you that the game is too difficult, or not challenging enough. Use your own judgment.

MAKE THE MOST OF THE IMPORTANT YEARS

The actual and deliberate attempt to educate babies is a revolutionary idea. It has always been accepted as fact that babies and toddlers soak up something from their environment, but we now know that this is the most important time in life for the child to acquire many basic learnings. We cannot leave these important years to chance. The activities given in this book can give your baby the intellectual stimulation so necessary to his future success in school. If you will consistently play with him in daily, well-planned lessons, you will prepare him for future learning and make the most of these important years. TEACH YOUR BABY!

CHAPTER II | PATTERNS OF GROWTH

THE DEVELOPMENT of infants has been studied in great detail, and the usual patterns of growth, or sequences of growth found in normal, healthy children, have frequently been described and charted. Even in children who happen to be relatively slow in development one finds patterns of growth that are similar to those in all children. However, variation in the rate of development may be great between children who are healthy and normal. Development may be rapid at times so that transitions in levels are not easily noticed. At other times it may be slower, and thus more obvious. However, all aspects of the sequences continue to be perfected and refined throughout childhood.

Development of Movement
Motor development starts at birth as the infant rotates his head and moves his arms and legs. When born, your baby cannot reach for objects, but he can see and hear. As he grows he becomes interested in bright-colored and noisy objects and he tries to reach for them. He starts by "reaching" with his eyes, while his arms move at random. Only later does he purposefully reach, first with his hand in a fisted position and later with his open hand.

Hand Movements
His grasp is crude and uncertain at first and he uses his full palm. He drops things when he wants to hold on to them,

and he does not know how to let go when he wants to pick up something else. It is only later that he learns how to release one object at will so that he may pick up another. The thumb and finger grasp develops after the palmer grasp. The child learns first to pick up an object with his thumb and *all* his fingers. Next he uses a few fingers and thumb, and finally only his thumb and index finger.

Other Body Movements

At the same time that the baby is learning to perfect the small motor movements—reaching, grasping and releasing—his body is becoming stronger and his larger muscle movements are developing. It is certain that the healthy baby will eventually stand in an erect posture and walk. There are individual differences in time and style schedules which each child goes through as he learns to walk upright like a man—but walk he does.

Various Levels of Development

Various parts of the body are in various motor levels at the same time. For example, a baby may be basically at the level of grasping while perfecting the previous level of releasing, and at the same time learning to crawl and/or to stand. In addition, his intellectual and language abilities are developing.

Intellectual Growth

The baby begins to understand cause-and-effect relationships—an early intellectual function—when he learns that he can move an object or produce a noise by striking a toy hanging over his crib. He learns that objects have names before he actually is able to say the names, and he babbles before he learns to say any real words as his language ability develops.

A Balance of Learned and Unlearned Skills

In following the program outlines in this book, it is necessary to try various activities to determine how to maintain a happy balance between keeping the lessons challenging enough to maintain interest and not making them so difficult as to be discouraging. You will want to encourage the further development of partially developed skills which your baby is able to accomplish with some ease, and also to concentrate on skills which the child does not have at all.

Fun for Your Baby, Fun for You

Your baby will learn best when you relate his own developmental levels to the activities given in the book. In matching the activities with your baby, use your own imagination and ingenuity. You cannot go wrong if you study what the baby is able to do, if you choose activities that fit him, and, above all, if both of you have fun. Overtiring and frustration (if either you or the baby gets angry) are signs that tell you to quit an activity for the present; you might want to pick up on it again in the future.

Children's Growth Rates Vary

The growth-pattern pictures that follow will help you to recognize easily some of the landmarks of typical sensori-motor development in the first three years of life. Since children vary widely in their style and time schedules of growth, I have not given ages for each picture. Although in the chapters that follow I have given ages in the chapter titles, these are to be considered approximations—that is, the activities suggested in each chapter are appropriate for babies at *about* the age stated. Developmental schedules are really models of the ideal child; no real child develops according to an abstract model. Therefore, do not be concerned if, on the one hand, your child seems "behind" the stated ages or, on the other, imagine you have a genius if he seems to be ahead.

GROWTH PATTERNS IN ORDER OF DEVELOPMENT

I. HEAD CONTROL

Lying on Back

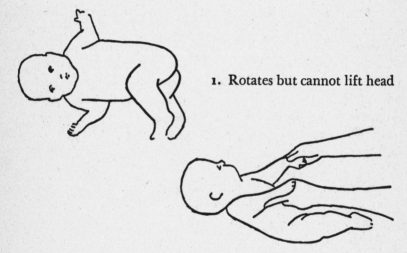

1. Rotates but cannot lift head

2. Head sags while baby is being pulled to sitting position

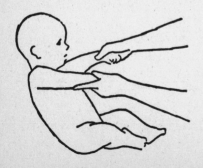

3. Head held steady while baby is being pulled to sitting position

Lying on Stomach

1. Cannot lift head

2. Begins to lift head

3. Lifts heads and shoulders
and rests on elbows

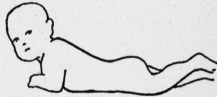

4. Straightens arms

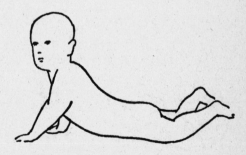

II. SITTING

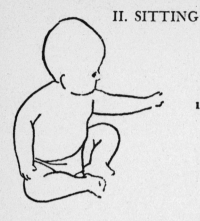

1. Balances when put into sitting position

2. Leans forward on hands

3. Sits firmly

III. LOCOMOTION

Rolling

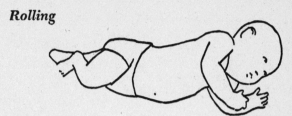

1. From back to stomach

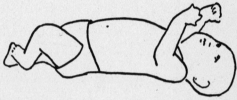

2. From stomach to back

Crawling (stomach contacts floor)

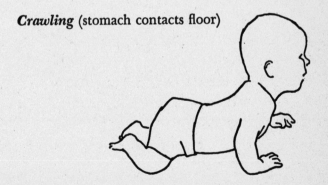

Creeping (stomach lifted, rests on feet, hands and knees)

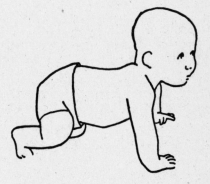

1. Rocks back and forth

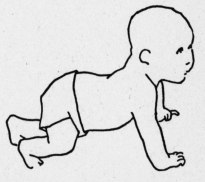

2. Moves forward

IV. STANDING

1. Bounces when hands are held

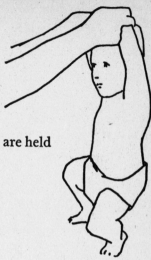

2. Pulls himself to feet

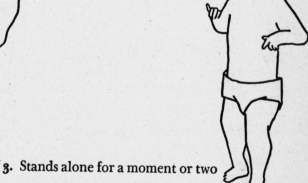

3. Stands alone for a moment or two

V. WALKING

1. Walks while
   two hands are held

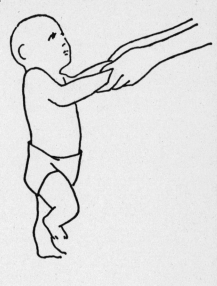

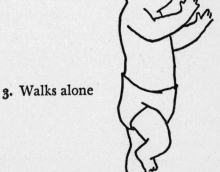

2. Walks while
   one hand is held

3. Walks alone

VI. REACHING, GRASPING, RELEASING

1. Hand fisted, grasps (without intention) adult's finger when placed in hand

2. Hand fisted, arms move aimlessly in any direction, "reaches" with eyes

3. Hand still fisted, still unable to reach, but places his fingers (with intention) around a stick or finger placed near his hand

4. Hand open, reaches, touches and pushes object (with intention)

5. Reaches for and grasps object crudely (it may drop out of his hand)

6. Reaches directly, grasps firmly with his full hand and is able to release an object (with intention)

VII. THUMB AND FINGER GRASPING

1. Using thumb and tips of all fingers, grasps and lifts object

2. With thumb, index and middle fingers only, picks up an object

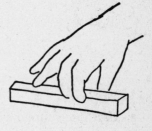

3. Using thumb and index finger, picks up an object about one inch in diameter

4. Using thumb and index finger, picks up an object about one-fourth inch in diameter

VIII. FINGER COORDINATION

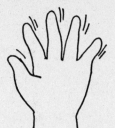

1. With some degree of control is able to move the fingers in many directions

2. Uses the index finger separately

3. Uses the thumb separately

IX. ARM COORDINATION

1. Using both arms, reaches and stretches in any direction

2. Using both arms, holds a large lightweight object

3. Using both arms and hands, holds an object with one hand so that he can perform a task with the other hand

4. Using both arms and hands, manipulates hands simultaneously

5. Using both arms and hands, alternates hands

X. EYE-HAND COORDINATION

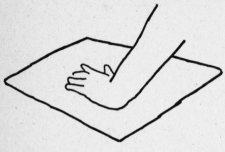

1. Controlling the arm, places hands within a large area

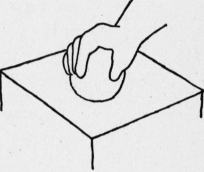

2. Places an object into a large area (box)

3. Puts a small object into a small area (nested cups)

4. Places a small object in an exact place

<table>
<tr><td>CHAPTER III</td><td></td></tr>
</table>

CHAPTER III | # HELPING YOUR BABY TO LEARN

EDUCATION for life, starting in infancy and continuing throughout the formative years, must include not only the acquisition of information but also the opportunity for the fullest development of the whole child—physical, intellectual, emotional and social. Education includes learning to get along well with others in the family and community; learning to trust and to love others, which will eventually lead to adjustment in love and marriage; learning to work with a sense of personal satisfaction and a feeling of contributing to the well-being of others; learning to face life with courage and actually to like oneself; and learning to see oneself as part of a larger, cosmic process. Being able to accomplish these "life tasks" leads to a feeling of adequacy.

The Importance of Security

Every child needs to feel secure. Security comes from a feeling of adequacy—"I am an OK person"—as well as from a feeling of belonging—"The family members like me and I like them; I belong to them and they belong to me." To become secure, the child must enter the family as a sharing rather than a helpless, receiving member. If the creation of a happy family group is to be achieved, each member must ask the question, "What can I give to our group?" as well as "What can I expect to receive from them?"

The child who feels adequate will be able to learn and to create. He will learn from his environment and he will give to his environment some of his own work with the stamp of his own personality. He will see himself as a part of our ever-changing world, and will be able to adjust to these changes, using his creative ability to solve problems that arise. This is truly the goal of education.

Your baby's early learning, from his environment and from the lessons you give him, will take him through his first years and also will allow him to go on to more advanced learning much more easily.

Early Forms of Learning

The baby will learn in these ways:

1. Trial and error. By giving him household items to manipulate by himself, he learns how they work through his own errors. For example, he might play by himself with nested cups and, by making many mistakes and correcting himself, discover that smaller cups go into larger ones, but not vice versa.

2. Imitation. Children learn a great deal by watching older children and adults. You can show a child how to do something and, if the task is not too complex for his abilities, he will learn how to do it by imitating you.

3. Natural consequences. The child also learns through the natural consequences of his own behavior. For example, if he touches something that is hot, he learns not to do it again because it hurts.

4. Logical consequences. Since some necessary lessons are too dangerous for us to allow the child to learn them through trial and error or natural consequences, we can set up logical consequences in the environment which can teach him. We can, for example, quietly take him into the house if he insists on straying off the sidewalk into the middle of the road. He can be given a chance to try to "play right" the next day. If mother is consistent and does not get angry, he will learn from the consequence of his behavior. Other logical consequences involve teaching the child the expectations of the home. For example, if the child dawdles a great deal at meals, the mother might take his plate of food away after an appropriate length of time; if he is still hungry, he will learn to eat more quickly next time. It is the parents' job to expose the child to experiences, not to shield him from them, to teach him to overcome difficulties, not to move difficulties out of his way. I mean, of course, difficulties and experiences which the child may reasonably be expected to be able to handle, such as normal, daily frustrations.

Your Attitude Toward His Learning

A cheerful, optimistic, friendly attitude toward the baby is important during your lessons. To encourage him to learn, he must feel good about himself and optimistic about his ability. He must have the courage to try new things. If he does not handle a task very well, you can encourage him to try again by showing faith in his abilities. As the teacher, you must be an enthusiastic believer in what the lessons can accomplish. If you are convinced that you can be the baby's teacher, you will enjoy the lessons and so will the baby.

Guidelines to the Daily Lessons

1. During the first few months you will not be able to spend more than the baby's short waking periods—perhaps a few minutes several times a day. As he gets older, plan fifteen-minute to half-hour lessons, and later, one-hour lessons. It is important that these lessons become part of a structured routine.

2. Choose a convenient time for you and the baby. He should be well rested, freshly diapered, and comfortable in general.

3. Choose one place for the lessons and use that same place every day. Activities for the first few months may be done in the crib, on the bath table, or on a blanket on the floor. Later a table is preferable to sitting on the floor because it establishes a working situation, good training for the school years ahead. For the baby who is beginning to sit, I suggest an infant seat such as a canvas seat within a large table area in which the baby can be strapped to help him sit. If you establish a daily time and specific place, it will be easier to teach your baby.

4. Your baby should be comfortably dressed in clothing that is not too heavy. The room should be warm but not hot. It should be quiet and free of distractions.

5. Toys that are used specifically for the daily lessons should be kept in a separate container (laundry basket or carton) out of the baby's reach at other times so that they will have special attraction for him.

6. A small box should be kept on the table to hold toys with many small parts, such as beads for stringing.

7. Be positive in your teaching. If you emphasize what your baby can do and realize that what he cannot do is unimportant, you are certain to encourage the child so that he will keep on trying. When you correct a mistake, do not make it seem important; simply show him the right way immediately by encouraging him and showing faith in his ability.

8. Keep a notebook of lesson plans. There are many activities to choose from in this book, and you needn't by any means use them all. Select the ones that seem the most enjoyable to you and which challenge your baby. Plan lessons ahead of time and keep notes on what worked, what did not, and what you think should be repeated. Young children like to do the same things over and over. However, your baby must also be given new things so that he does not develop a rigid adherence to tasks that he finds familiar and easy. You will find your own system for balancing old activities with new and will sense when to go faster to include more activities in one sitting and when to slow down.

9. It is necessary to expand his attention span so that he will work for a long time on the same thing. Show him different ways to play with the same toy, but be sure to allow him to explore new ways for himself.

10. Show him one toy at a time. Put it back in the box before giving him another. When he gets a little older, let him put the toy back into the box himself.

11. Break each task to be learned into steps. For example, when giving the child nested cups to put together, first give him two, and when he masters these, give him three, and so on.

12. Stop the lesson while it is still fun, before the baby becomes tired and fusses. Next time he will want more.

13. When a task becomes a chore, work on it for only a short time. If it is too difficult, drop it for a day or a week, or even a month, before trying it again.

14. Remember that you are the teacher and must teach according to your lesson plans. Do not let the child control the situation and tell you which toys he will play with. If you have taken out a puzzle and he then gets a whim to blow bubbles, you can firmly promise that he may blow bubbles just as soon as he is finished with the puzzle. Be quietly firm, not angry, do not say it more than once, and be sure to keep your promise. He will learn that he cannot always have his own way, and also that he has some choice and that you are not stubborn.

15. If the child gets angry for any reason and begins to have a temper tantrum, or simply cries, or is irritable, put away the toys for the day, and work again the next day. You must not be angry yourself or begin a power contest between you in which you say, "You do as I say or else!" and he says, "I don't have to." Keep your cool and have a smile on your face. He will learn from the consequence of the situation, but he will not learn by punishment.

16. He will enjoy his lesson time with you and may cry when it ends. Do not continue because he demands this. Just put him in his playpen and give him a toy to play with by himself. He will gradually learn that there are times that he plays with you and times that he plays alone, and that both are pleasurable.

17. Do not compare your baby with others. Each child

does things in his own way and in his own time. Comparisons are dangerous. If you even think, "He is not doing as well as so-and-so," he will know that you do not have faith in him and he will lose faith in himself. It is important, therefore, that you yourself genuinely appreciate your baby's individuality in size and timing and that you be free of anxiety about how he compares with others.

18. Encouragement is the key to good teaching. A child who is encouraged keeps trying even after doing poorly, but do not give constant and meaningless praise. Then a child works only for adult praise. He should work because he receives satisfaction in accomplishment. *Comment on his accomplishment*—"That is a pretty picture; you must have enjoyed making it." *Do not give praise* to have him do things only to please you—"You are a good boy to make a nice picture."

19. I strongly urge you to organize a few parents in a study group to discuss the lessons in this book, and ideas relating to them. Some books that would give additional help are:

Beecher, M. and W., *Parents on the Run*. New York: Julian Press, 1955.

Dreikurs, R., and Grey, L., *A Parent's Guide to Child Discipline*. New York: Hawthorn Books, Inc., 1970.

Dreikurs, R., and Soltz, V., *Children: the Challenge*. New York: Hawthorn Books, Inc., 1964.

Glasser, W., *Schools Without Failure*. New York: Harper and Row, 1969.

Rasey, M., and Menge, J. W., *What We Learn from Children*. New York: Harper and Brothers, 1956.

Various authors, *Articles of Supplementary Reading for Parents*. Chicago: Alfred Adler Institute of Chicago, 1970. (Available from Alfred Adler Institute, 110 South Dearborn Avenue, Chicago, Illinois 60603.)

Activity Programs

NEWBORN
TO SITTING

CHAPTER IV | # ACTIVITY PROGRAMS— NEWBORN TO ONE MONTH

THE NEWBORN's major job is simply getting used to his existence in the wide world outside the womb. All of his physical functions must make an adaptation from the confines and protection of his mother's uterus to the openness of his new environment. Unless he has colic or is excessively irritable, the newborn sleeps most of the time and cries mainly because of hunger. Typically, he has seven or eight short waking periods and falls back to sleep while being fed.

As long as the baby is making physical adjustments, he is not ready for a great amount of social stimulation. It is best to let him have all the sleep he needs, and he should not, therefore, be overstimulated with a great deal of play. The following are suggestions for limited sensory stimulation which, unless overdone, will not interfere with his adjustment to his new home. Use your own good judgment and remember he must sleep a lot. Don't awaken him to teach him or to play. During his first month of family living, the best time to teach him through play is when he is being changed and after feedings.

Stimulate Feeling
1. Shift his position. The baby may be placed on his stomach as well as on his back

2. While on the changing table, he can be gently massaged for short periods on his stomach, back, shoulders, arms and legs.

3. Cuddle him and hold him firmly.

4. Rock him a little while you hold him.

Stimulate Seeing

1. Shift him to another side of the crib when you put him down so that the light can excite each eye.

2. Attach a bright toy to the side of the crib toward which his head is turned. At this age he will not see toys hung over the middle of the bed because he keeps his head to one side. The toy should be at least twelve inches from the bridge of his nose (he will not be able to see it if the toy is much closer). If the baby is awake, shake the toy so it will attract his attention. An irregular shape is more attractive and noticeable to a very young baby than a smooth shape. A multicolored paper party toy may be used, or you can attach colorful, crumpled aluminum foil to a stick. You might use several toys, of different shapes and colors, for variation.

Stimulate Hearing

1. Sing to him or say a nursery rhyme.

2. Let a radio play in his room for a short time.

3. Play a record or tape in his room for a short time. Caution: Do not play music constantly. We tend to "tune out" sounds that we hear constantly.

Stimulate Generally

1. Be quietly friendly with him; enjoy how he feels when you hold him and allow your enjoyment to show on your face. Relax—he isn't that fragile!

2. Enjoy giving him his bath, and he will enjoy it too. It will be easier on you if you use the washbowl or a fabric baby tub at a comfortable height than if you bend down to use the regular tub.

3. Take him outdoors for a period each day when your doctor says that he is old enough. The time for outings varies with the season, the baby's weight and the doctor's viewpoint.

4. During the day, shift his crib to another part of the room. Don't keep the house quiet. He will learn to sleep with sound, and it will seem friendly to him when he awakens.

SAMPLE DAILY ACTIVITY PROGRAMS—Newborn to One Month

Your baby's feedings, clothing changes, and bathings will, in themselves, be more stimulation than he ever had before birth. It is wise to select mostly from activities that can be included along with his living routines. For example, while he is sleeping, you can change his position in the crib in relation to the window so that each eye can be excited by the daylight when he awakens. You might place him on one side of his crib after a feeding and on the other side after the next feeding. This stimulation, tailored to his sleeping routine, will thus not overtire him. His bath will stimulate his entire body. The following daily activity programs are given as suggestions. Each program can be continued for several days and activities for one day can be continued or interchanged with those of another day. Use your own judgment by selecting an activity from each category, trying them and observing whether or not the baby enjoys them. Above all, do not tire him.

> *Activities are listed* briefly *in these examples of how you might put together a daily activity program for your baby. These same activities are often described in greater detail on the preceding pages, and there you will find, under the following categories, many more activities to choose from to give your baby's daily program variety and interest.*
> *Stimulate Feeling, page 59*
> *Stimulate Seeing, page 60*
> *Stimulate Hearing, page 60*
> *Stimulate Generally, page 61*

Daily Program I

STIMULATE FEELING
√ Shift his position from stomach to back

STIMULATE SEEING
√ Shift him to another side of his crib so light can excite each eye

STIMULATE HEARING
√ Sing to him as you diaper him

STIMULATE GENERALLY
√ Be quietly friendly with him and enjoy how he feels as you hold him

Daily Program II

STIMULATE FEELING
√ As you diaper him, gently massage him

STIMULATE SEEING
√ Shift him to another side of crib so light can excite each eye

STIMULATE HEARING
√ Let a radio play in his room for a short time

STIMULATE GENERALLY
√ Enjoy giving him his bath

Daily Program III

STIMULATE FEELING
√ Shift his position from stomach to back
√ Cuddle him and hold him firmly

STIMULATE SEEING
√ Shift him to another side of the crib so light can excite each eye

STIMULATE HEARING
√ Play a record for him

STIMULATE GENERALLY
√ Shift his crib to another part of the room

Daily Program IV

STIMULATE FEELING
√ Rock him while you hold him

STIMULATE SEEING
√ Shift him to another side of the crib so light can excite
   each eye
√ Attach a bright toy to the side of his crib

STIMULATE HEARING
√ Say a nursery rhyme to him

STIMULATE GENERALLY
√ Take him outdoors

CHAPTER V | ACTIVITY PROGRAMS—
ONE TO THREE MONTHS

BY THE TIME the baby is one month old his muscles are firmer, his movements are more coordinated, and he seems less fragile to you. He responds quite happily when he is comfortable and lets you know when he is uncomfortable. That is, he is quite happy when his stomach is full and he is dry; but he will certainly let you know by crying when he is hungry. A wet or dirty diaper may or may not bother him.

He still sleeps much of the time but is a little more alert when awake. He usually has five or six feeding periods during the day and will still frequently drop off to sleep while feeding. He stares at the window if his head faces it; the light attracts his attention but he probably does not actually "see a window." He enjoys the sound of voices and being cuddled. He may enjoy his bath but resist or fuss when being dressed and undressed. It will be easiest for you and for him if you select clothing that does not have to go on over his head.

He may cry even after you have given him his necessary care and have cuddled him and shown him your love. It is best not to play the game of picking him up to quiet his crying. He will soon learn, if he is not picked up, that there are better ways of getting his parents' attention—cooing, smiling, and the like. There is a prevalent opinion among physicians and psychologists that crying does not hurt the baby. He will learn to cry less when you respond less to his crying; and he will become pleasant when you respond to his pleasantness.

The activities presented in this chapter are suggested for the baby from one month old to roughly three months, or whenever he is able to move on to those suggested in the next chapter. You can continue for a while some of the activities of Chapter IV and later start some in Chapter VI while still working on those in this chapter. Remember, do not disturb the baby's sleep to play with and educate him. He still needs much rest. Some activities are listed in more than one teaching category. For example, play with a rattle stimulates seeing *and* hearing.

Stimulate Feeling

1. Continue the massaging and shifting positions of Chapter IV.

2. While the baby is on his back, move his arms over his head and back to place.

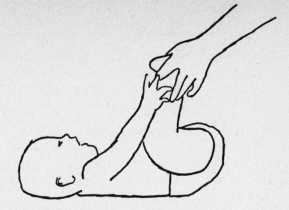

3. While he is on his back, push his legs up to a knee-bend and back to place.

4. While he is on his stomach, push gently against his feet.

Stimulate Seeing

1. When on his stomach, he will see more as he is increasingly able to lift his head and stay awake for longer periods. Place him on his stomach for periods, after removing his crib bumpers so that they do not block his view.

2. Occasionally put a patterned sheet on his bed and bumpers for added visual stimulation while he is on his stomach.

3. Hang bright objects from the side of the crib.

4. Hang bright objects across the crib.

5. Hang a mobile across the crib.

6. Move a small flashlight in front of him slowly, in a 180° arc. See if he can follow it with his eyes. You will have to try this from various distances until you find the best distance for his eyes. He may follow the light with jerky movements at first; later he will follow it smoothly. (At first he probably will not be able to see things that are close to him. Try shaking an object at various levels from twelve to thirty-six inches from the bridge of his nose until he fixes his eyes upon it.)

7. Use a toy in the same manner as the flashlight.

8. Allow the toy to disappear from his line of vision and then to reappear. You may have to shake the toy in front of his eyes if he does not pay attention to its reappearance. Eventually he will learn to keep his eyes on the point of disappearance and wait for the toy to reappear.

9. Cut a six- to eight-inch bright red paper circle and paste it on a white twelve- to sixteen-inch paper square. Bring it into his line of sight from twelve to thirty-six inches from the bridge of his nose. Shake it until he watches it. Then move it slowly in a 180° arc from side to side. Also move it over his head and downward toward his toes.

10. Hold a multicolored paper toy or homemade version (see Chapter IV, page 60) in his line of vision. Shake it, starting at twelve to thirty-six inches, until he watches it. Then try bringing it closer to him. See if he will watch the toy when it is about six inches from his nose.

11. Using ink or pencil draw diagonal lines across a two-inch-square cardboard. On another two-inch square draw a bull's-eye with concentric circles. Attach each to a stick and show them one at a time to the baby. Try them at various distances from his eyes until he is able to fix on them.

12. Move his hands in front of his face so that he can see his hands and their movement. Put his hands together in front of his eyes and then pull them apart.

13. Put a small lightweight rattle in his hand; later put it in his other hand. Eventually he will learn to see the toys held in his own hand. NOTE: When the baby gets a little older and notices you more often than the object, stand aside so that he sees the object but is not distracted by you.

Stimulate Hearing

1. Tie a little bell on each bootie. He will hear the sound as he moves his legs.

2. Put a lightweight rattle in his hand. As he moves his hand (involuntarily at first, later with intention) the rattle will make a sound.

3. Play a radio, tape, phonograph, music box, or the TV for him—but not for long periods of time.

4. Talk and sing while cuddling him.

5. Let him hear the sound of a metronome or clock tick for short periods.

6. Talk to him from different places of the room. See if he hears and follows with his eyes. If he does both, it heralds the beginning of the coordination of sound and visual image.

7. Ring a small bell occasionally from different parts of the room.

Stimulate Generally

1. He will respond to smiling and talking and will actually start smiling to himself sometime between one month and three months. Continue the suggestions for general stimulation set forth in Chapter IV as you start on those in Chapter V.

2. Change and feed him from alternate sides.

3. Place him in a playpen every day for a little while so that he will get used to it, in preparation for the months ahead.

4. Place him nearby for some family meals (if he is awake).

5. Place him in the kitchen occasionally while you prepare meals.

6. Take him outdoors in his carriage for walks.

7. Take him for car rides.

8. Take him with you when visiting friends.

The activities in this chapter should be continued until the baby rotates his head freely from side to side when he is on his back, holds his head quite steady when propped up in a sitting position, watches his hands clasped together over the center of his body when on his back, and crudely grasps objects.

SAMPLE DAILY ACTIVITY PROGRAMS—One to Three Months

As during his first month, the baby will still sleep much of the time, but his periods of wakefulness will increase. It is wisest to choose only a few activities during the day since the baby still needs much rest and should not be over-stimulated. The following are some suggestions for daily programs—but they are only suggestions, and you will want to make up your own programs to suit you and your baby.

> *Activities are listed* briefly *in these examples of how you might put together a daily activity program for your baby. These same activities are often described in greater detail on the preceding pages, and there you will find, under the following categories, many more activities to choose from to give your baby's daily program variety and interest.*
> *Stimulate Feeling, page 66*
> *Stimulate Seeing, page 67*
> *Stimulate Hearing, page 69*
> *Stimulate Generally, page 70*

Daily Program I

STIMULATE FEELING
√ Massage and shift positions

STIMULATE SEEING
√ Remove crib bumpers so he can see

STIMULATE HEARING
√ Tie a bell on bootie

STIMULATE GENERALLY
√ Place him in playpen

Daily Program II

STIMULATE FEELING
√ Move his arms over head and back

STIMULATE SEEING
√ Place a patterned sheet on bed

STIMULATE HEARING
√ Put a rattle in his hand

STIMULATE GENERALLY
√ Change and feed him from alternate sides

Daily Program III

STIMULATE FEELING
√ Continue massage
√ Push his legs up to knee-bend position

STIMULATE SEEING
√ Place bright objects on side of crib

STIMULATE HEARING
√ Play radio, phonograph, or tape

STIMULATE GENERALLY
√ Place him nearby at family meals

Daily Program IV

STIMULATE FEELING
√ Push gently against his feet

STIMULATE SEEING
√ Hang bright objects across crib

STIMULATE HEARING
√ Play radio, phonograph or tape
√ Let him hear a metronome or clock

STIMULATE GENERALLY
√ Place him in playpen

Daily Program V

STIMULATE FEELING
✓ Push his legs to a knee-bend position
✓ Continue the massage and shifting positions

STIMULATE SEEING
✓ Hang a mobile across the crib

STIMULATE HEARING
✓ Let him hear a metronome or clock

STIMULATE GENERALLY
✓ Take him outdoors

Daily Program VI

STIMULATE FEELING
✓ Push gently against his feet

STIMULATE SEEING
✓ Allow toy to disappear from his line of vision and then to reappear

STIMULATE HEARING
✓ Tie a bell on bootie

STIMULATE GENERALLY
✓ Visit friends with baby

CHAPTER VI | # ACTIVITY PROGRAMS—
FOUR TO FIVE MONTHS

Now THE BABY is able to hold his head quite steady when he is propped up in sitting position, surrounded by pillows, placed in a canvas chair with belt, or held in an adult's lap. His newest way of learning about the world now includes touching everything within reach and bringing it to his mouth. He has discovered his hands, which are no longer mostly fisted. He is able to bring them together over his chest, and he spends a lot of time looking at his fingers and hands and putting them in his mouth. He is beginning to learn that toys and fingers are different things—seeing and tasting them make this clearer to him. He is now able to turn his whole body toward a toy which he sees in order to reach

for it, but he will grasp it crudely and may drop it immediately. Instead of crying for food immediately upon awakening, he often babbles to himself and he usually gets through a feeding without falling asleep. In play he uses his growing sensorimotor skills—see and move, hear and move, feel and move, and so forth—and he may play quite happily by himself for a while. It is very important to allow him time to himself for self-exploration and sensorimotor practice as well as the special time when you play to teach him. In other words, put toys over his crib and within his reach when he is on the floor or in his playpen, and let him play by himself for a while.

Scheduling Play

This age is a good one for starting a regular scheduled educational playtime for you and the baby. Pick one spot in the house as a special teaching place. You can now prop the baby up with pillows and sit on the floor with him or strap him in a canvas chair or baby chair-table. Ten to fifteen minutes will probably be long enough to be fun and interesting for him without being tiring. You can give him another such playtime later in the day if you wish. He may

cry when you want to leave or put him to bed, but don't let his tears tyrannize you. If you set the time limits and go about your own business after the play period, he will learn that crying doesn't make you dance to his tune and that he had better stop crying and do something which is more fun, like playing with toys all by himself. He will learn to play alone very happily for longer periods; in this way you will train him to be less dependent upon you, and he will start taking responsibility for his *own* well-being.

Stimulate Feeling

1. Rub body parts with soft silk or a feather; name parts of body as you rub. He will not be able to say the names but he will begin to learn the sounds of the words and later know that the sound goes with the part.

2. Rub body parts with terry cloth so that he can feel a contrasting rough texture.

3. Give him a soft plastic "clutch ball" to grasp and let go of.

4. Give him a clean spoon to hold and put in his mouth. He will like to feel the shape of it in his hand and in his mouth.

5. Give him a small soft rag doll to clutch, release and feel.

6. Give him things of different textures to touch: smooth plastic, rough towel, sticky tape, feather, sponge, pot scraper, aluminum foil, wax paper, tissue paper.

7. Give him a large plastic ring to feel.

Stimulate Seeing

1. While he is on his back, put a toy (rattle, small soft-plastic toy) *near* his hand when he is looking at his hand. See if he looks at the toy, then back at his hand, and finally clutches the toy and brings it to his mouth.

2. While he is on his back, put a toy *in* his hand when he is not looking at his hand. See if he notices it and brings it to his mouth.

3. While he is on his back, show him a toy when he is *not* looking at his hand (don't place it in his hand) and see if he reaches for it. He may first bring his hand up so he can see it, look at his hand, and then reach for the toy.

4. Hang a cradle gym or other hanging toy over his crib so that he can reach for it and play without anyone's help.

5. Suspend a rattle across his crib. Attach a string to it and shake it so that it makes a noise. Then put the string in his hand. See if he pulls it to repeat the noise.

6. Do the same with a bell.

7. Attach a balloon to his wrist with a string so that he can watch it.

8. While he is on his back, show him a rattle. Move the rattle toward his hand so that he can grasp it. You can say, "Get the rattle," as you move it toward him. He will not understand the words now but will begin to hear words as you show him their meanings.

9. While he is on his stomach, dangle a rattle or other sound toy in front of his eyes. Raise the toy slowly and see if he raises his head and shoulders to follow the toy. You can say, "See the rattle."

10. He will quite naturally play with his feet when he is lying on his back but you can help him get started by playing with his feet and then putting them up so he sees them and reaches for them.

11. Give him a toy, to play with in his playpen, that he can push over and that will always return to upright position.

12. Let him hold his own bottle while feeding.

Stimulate Hearing

1. Crumple paper and let him hear the sound.

2. When outdoors in autumn, crumple leaves.

3. Attach bells to his booties so he will notice his feet and reach for them.

4. Play the radio, tapes, music box or TV for him for short periods.

5. Ring a bell from different parts of the room when he is not watching you. He will turn to find out where the sound comes from.

6. When you play on the floor with him or when he is in bed, stay behind him and shake a rattle a little to his right but behind him. Wait for him to look for the rattle. Repeat this on his left and directly in back of his head.

7. Repeat nursery rhymes or poems as you march around the room while carrying him. He will enjoy the movement and rhythm even if he does not understand the words.

8. He will enjoy the sound of a set of Japanese wind bells (small rectangles of glass that make a pleasant sound when the wind blows on them) hung near a window or doorway that receives a gentle breeze.

Stimulate Generally

1. Let him play by himself in his playpen for a while several times a day. He must learn to explore on his own and he must be given the time to do it. Give him some of the things to play with suggested in this chapter and in earlier ones.

2. Let him play on the floor for a while in various rooms of the house.

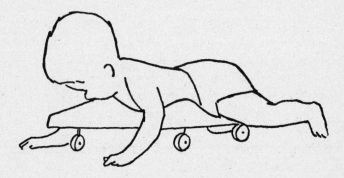

3. If you can, buy him a "crawligator" (plastic form with casters which holds baby's body as he wheels around on the floor). This can be given to him before he has the strength in his muscles actually to crawl.

4. When he is on his back, grasp his hands and gently pull him to sitting position.

5. Sing a song and hold him firmly around the middle; gently bounce him so that his feet touch the floor or bed. He will enjoy this kind of dancing.

6. Before falling asleep he will usually play for a while with his hands and feet or with the bedclothes. You might hang a cradle gym across his bed at this time.

7. Let him have fun in his bath. He will love to kick and splash. Prop his head up on a small sponge pillow or pad of folded diapers.

8. Take him for a ride in his carriage or for a visit to friends. He will notice many more things now than he did before.

9. Let him play in his playpen, crib or chair near older children. He will enjoy seeing them play and they will enjoy him too. He may cry when they leave but don't let it bother you. He will go back to playing by himself if you are not concerned.

Stimulate Imitation, the Beginning of Speech

We usually think that a baby begins to learn to speak when he is about a year old. However, he is actually learning about *how* to speak from the moment of the birth cry. For the first few weeks his crying seems always to sound the same, except that it may vary in volume. Pretty soon, mother is able to tell by the sound of his crying what it means: whether he is hungry or whether he is uncomfortable because he needs a diaper change. He is learning about *how* to speak by feeling the air flow in and out of his throat, nose, and mouth and he is learning to change from loud squalling to weak whimpering. As he sucks, swallows, belches and gurgles, he is practicing the movements needed in speaking. And, most important of all, he is learning that crying can be useful in getting him what he wants—he is learning to communicate. Most babies learn only too well to cry for things, and they continue to do so as they get older. The wise parent teaches the baby through her reaction that she is not so impressed with crying, and so trains him to communicate in other ways.

When he feels good after a meal, the baby starts to coo and, as he gets older, he babbles; he plays at speaking. But he first tells you things and understands you best through gestures. For example, when you tell him, "Eat more," he understands by your gestures rather than by the words you use.

During his first year the baby's life is full of imitation. Baby imitates parents and parents imitate baby. This is the beginning of speech. When mother smiles, he smiles back. When he coos, mother makes his sounds. When mother coos words of love, he coos back. He may not make the same sound in his cooing, but it is *his* beginning of speech. The following activities are suggested for teaching baby to imitate your movements and sounds; they should be undertaken only when he is contented, babbling a little, and actually paying attention to you. He may either lie on his back or be tied firmly in a canvas chair when engaging in these activities.

1. Move your finger in front of his face so that he follows your finger with his eyes.

2. Holding your finger in front of your own face, turn your head from right to left. When you catch his eye, drop your finger. See if he then moves his head back and forth as you do. Give him time to imitate; he probably needs more time than you think.

3. When he is able to imitate your head movement, stop and suddenly smile. See if he smiles back. Give him plenty

of time. Do not tickle or talk to him to get him to smile. You simply want him to *imitate* smiling. When he does smile, stop smiling, but look pleasant for about five seconds and then smile again. Do this only a few times. Do not try to force smiling; it won't work. If you enjoy this type of play, he will too.

4. Suddenly smile and make *one* sound that you have heard him say, such as a hard *g* or *r* sound (like gargling), or an *ah, uh* or *eh* sound. Do not say a lot of different sounds— just one at a time, the simpler, the better. Wait for him to imitate. Give him time; sit and look pleasant for at least five seconds before saying one of his sounds again. Sometimes he will imitate and put on a good show; at other times he will not even bother. If he does not imitate sounds after you try a few, stop and try again another day.

NOTE: He very likely will imitate your sounds for a few months and then stop imitating speech for several months because he just wants to listen. At such times he is learning about your speech even if he doesn't say things back to you. You can best help him during this time by saying a very few simple words—and the same one for each activity—so that he is not confused. For example, when you put him in his bath, say "Bath." When you feed him, say "Eat," or "Eat now." He may not repeat what you say, but he is learning anyway. At these times, he may imitate movements like waving "bye-bye." He may simply babble when he is all alone, but not talk at all when he is with you

SAMPLE DAILY ACTIVITY PROGRAMS—Four to Five Months

In order to give each baby the proper activities for his tastes and for his developmental levels, I have suggested in the preceding pages more activities than the individual parent will want or need to use. Choose at least one from each area of training (feeling, seeing, hearing, etc.) each day. Repeat those your baby likes and those you think he still needs to practice. Use some activities in his solitary play and some in his structured lessons. Introduce a new activity as well. If you find one too difficult, stop and try it again in the future.

Activities are listed briefly in these examples of how you might put together a daily activity program for your baby. These same activities are often described in greater detail on the preceding pages, and there you will find, under the following categories, many more activities to choose from to give your baby's daily program variety and interest.

Stimulate Feeling, page 76
Stimulate Seeing, page 77
Stimulate Hearing, page 78
Stimulate Generally, page 79
Stimulate Imitation, page 80

Daily Program I

STIMULATE FEELING
√ Rub body parts with silk or a feather

STIMULATE SEEING
√ Put a toy near his hand while he is looking at his hand

STIMULATE HEARING
√ Crumple paper so he can hear it

STIMULATE GENERALLY
√ Play in playpen

Daily Program II

STIMULATE FEELING
√ Rub body parts with silk or feather
√ Give him "clutch ball" to grasp

STIMULATE SEEING
√ Put a toy near his hand while he is looking at his hand
√ Put a toy near his hand when he is *not* looking at his hand

STIMULATE HEARING
√ Crumple leaves
√ Attach bells to bootie

STIMULATE GENERALLY
√ Play in playpen
√ Gently pull to sitting position

Daily Program III

STIMULATE FEELING
√ Rub body parts with terry cloth

STIMULATE SEEING
√ Put a string in his hand which is attached to a rattle

STIMULATE HEARING
√ Play the radio, tapes or TV

STIMULATE GENERALLY
√ Place him on a "crawligator"

STIMULATE IMITATION
√ Move your finger in front of his face
√ With your finger in front of your face, turn your head from left to right

Daily Program IV

STIMULATE FEELING
√ Give him a "clutch ball" to grasp
√ Give him a spoon to hold in his mouth

STIMULATE SEEING
√ Attach a balloon to his wrist
√ Put a toy in his hand when he is not looking

STIMULATE HEARING
√ Shake a rattle behind him to his right, then to his left

STIMULATE GENERALLY
√ Let him have fun in his bath

STIMULATE IMITATION
√ Smile at him, see if he smiles back

Daily Program V

STIMULATE FEELING
√ Give him different textures to touch

STIMULATE SEEING
√ Help him play with his feet

STIMULATE HEARING
√ Repeat nursery rhymes as you carry him and march with him

STIMULATE GENERALLY
√ Gently bounce him

STIMULATE IMITATION

√ Move your finger in front of his face

√ With your finger in front of your face, turn your head from left to right

Daily Program VI

STIMULATE FEELING

√ Give him plastic ring to feel

STIMULATE SEEING

√ Give him a toy to push over that will return to upright position

STIMULATE HEARING

√ Let him hear sound of Japanese wind bells

STIMULATE GENERALLY

√ Let him play near older children

STIMULATE IMITATION

√ Say a sound he is able to say and see if he imitates

Activity Programs

SITTING
TO TODDLING

CHAPTER VII | ACTIVITY PROGRAMS— SIX TO EIGHT MONTHS

THE ACTIVITIES in this chapter are to be used from the time the baby is on the verge of sitting alone through to his mastery of sitting alone well. At first, when he sits alone, he will often use his hands to help balance himself. He enjoys sitting up because he is getting more control of his muscles. He is on his way to the upright posture of adults, but it will still be some months before he actually stands.

He was "reaching out" with his eyes to see things in the last period. Now he is "hungry" to touch things. He will reach and strain to hold whatever he sees and to touch and taste it with his mouth and tongue. He likes to explore a toy completely by looking at it, feeling it, mouthing it and banging it—a clothespin will do for this kind of play, or a rattle or squeak toy. In this way he is learning about the size, shape, weight, sound, texture and taste of things.

He is also beginning to see spatial relationships—how far away a toy is from him and how far away it is from another toy. When he drops a toy, he leans over and stretches to get it. He may overreach and correct his error by pulling back to get it. Thus he learns to judge where things are in space.

His hands are no longer fisted. He is beginning to use his thumb, but his grasp is still crude compared with the way it will be a few months from now. He is still more expert with his eyes than with his hands. He will look at and study a small object but be unable to pick it up easily. Larger things (size of a one-inch block) he can pick up more easily. He can hold two toys, one in each hand, at the same time.

He now makes a variety of vowel and consonant sounds (*ma, mu, da, e, b*). He is quite sociable and likes to be with other family members. Toward the end of this period he will be able to play simple games such as patty-cake and bye-bye. Although he likes to have people around him, he will play by himself if he is allowed to do so.

Baby's structured playtime should be lengthened to a half-hour period at one time; you can play with him at two different play periods in one day if you find it fun and if it does not interfere with his sleep and his time to play by himself. Choose from the activities in this chapter and continue some of those from the last chapter which are still fun and challenging. Have a regular playtime each day at the same time. This will help him begin to learn about time and order.

He should continue to play by himself a good deal of the time, exploring on his own and thinking of ways to entertain himself. He should spend some time each day in his playpen so that he is used to its being a *good* place to be. You can catch up with your own work at these times. Mothers, too, have rights, and working without children under foot is one of them.

At about this age, he may start being shy of people whom

he does not know. Do not let this keep people away from your home. Just ask them not to rush to grab him and not to pay too much attention to him at first. It takes a little while for him to get acquainted. Simply let him get used to other people; don't decide that he only wants you and that strangers are bad for him. He should learn to get along with other people and know that they are his friends.

As usual, use your own judgment as to which activities are fun and challenging. If he gives up easily, encourage his trying to work out the problem so that he learns that if he "tries" he can do well. At these times you can give him a little help, without actually doing the task for him or forcing him to do it. Coercion can start a power struggle between the two of you which is of no use in teaching him, nor indeed in your relationship in general. You can change activities as often in a play period as you think necessary. However, if you encourage him to play as long as possible with one thing, his attention span will increase. Since he is still very young and can get overexcited quite easily, he should not receive too much noisy and exciting stimulation at one time.

Stimulate Seeing

1. Let him play with ordinary household items: pots and pans, spoons, cups, hairbrush, magazines, cards, bottle covers, cloth, door stops, and others. He will like to explore these objects and will learn something about them. Tell him the names of the objects, even though he cannot say words.

2. Place a device over his crib that reacts when he pulls or grabs parts (bells ring or a wood block beats against another piece of wood). He learns cause-effect relationships and learns to "solve problems."

3. Place floating toys in his bath water. He will enjoy them and will see that some things float in water.

4. Give him a clean clothespin to play with. He will love to mouth it and bang it on the table.

5. Place toys in various positions and distances from him so that he has to reach for them. Do not always place them in his hands. Say "Get the block" (or whatever the object may be).

6. Give him a mirror so that he can see his own image. He will also see reflections of other things. Show him his eyes, nose, mouth, etc., saying their names. Show him your eyes, nose, mouth, too. Let him compare the reflection of your face with your actual face.

7. Help him develop eye-hand coordination by encouraging him to change a toy or spoon from one hand to the other.

Put his left hand on the toy while he holds it in his right hand. See if he will change hands. Try the same thing reversing hands. Show him how to do it.

8. Give him a small block to hold in each hand. See if he will drop one of the blocks when you give him a third block. If he gets angry and cries, he probably does not know how to do this. Show him how by taking one block out of his hand and giving him another.

9. Drop a small block on his table. See if he will reach for it. At first he may reach too far because he still has to learn how far away things are from him.

10. Let him feed himself bits of food with his fingers.

11. He will be able to take off his booties and stockings. This is good practice for future dressing. If he takes them off when you think he needs the booties for warmth, just tie a double bow so that he cannot untie them. Later, untie them and let him take them off when you change him.

12. Play peek-a-boo with toys. Let things appear and disappear.

13. Cover his eyes with his own hands so that he learns to play peek-a-boo. Say "Peek-a-boo" as you take his hands away from his eyes. He will learn to do this by himself. Then cover your own eyes and, when you take your hands away, say "Peek-a-boo."

14. He probably will start to throw things on the floor while sitting at his table and expect you to pick them up so that he can throw them on the floor again. Playing this "game" trains him to think you should give him service. If he throws toys on the floor, do not scold; merely take them away quietly and let him sit without toys for a few minutes. He will learn that this is not the way to play at his table. Try again. If he again throws, stop the lesson and try again the following day. You must train him to play properly. He can practice throwing things when he is on the floor and can retrieve them by himself.

15. Give him a metal, plastic or enamel cup with a handle. Place it upside down on his table and see if he turns it over. If he doesn't, show him how.

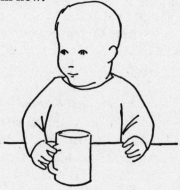

16. Give him a small amount of dry cereal in a plastic bottle about two to three inches high and one and a half inches in diameter. Shake the bottle so that he sees the cereal, and give it to him to play with. See if he turns it upside down to allow the cereal to fall out. If he does not, do it for him. At first he probably will not see the cereal fall out because he will watch only the bottle, which is larger. As you play this game, he will learn to watch the cereal and eventually will put it back in the bottle or eat it.

17. Put a small (size of a pea) piece of cracker or cereal on his table. At first he will be able to put his hand on it but not to pick it up. You can help him by putting his thumb and forefinger on it with your fingers on top of his.

18. Tie a string on a three- to four-inch ring (embroidery hoop will do). Putting the ring out of his reach on the table, give him the string. Show him how to get the ring if he needs help.

19. Show him realistic pictures of objects. He will probably try to pick up the objects at first; he will soon learn that a picture of an object is not the object itself.

Stimulate Hearing

1. Let him shake a rattle, rustle tissue paper or aluminum foil, tear paper and crumble dry leaves.

2. Give him a plastic squeak toy. At first, he may turn around to see what makes the noise until he learns that his squeezing the toy does it. He will learn something about cause-and-effect relationships.

3. Give him blocks with bells to play with.

4. Play the radio, tapes and phonograph for him.

5. Give him a bell on a handle. He will shake the handle

and ring the bell. He will also see the "clapper" and play with it; later he will learn that it is the "clapper" that makes the sound.

6. While he is sitting in his chair, hold a bell or rattle behind him to the right and ring it. Ask him, "Where is the bell?" See if he will turn his whole body around to find it. Play the game to his left also.

7. Call his attention to the sound of running water, footsteps, a closing door and other household sounds.

8. The first time he experiences the sound of thunder, he may be startled. Smile and say "Bang, bang," and give him his clothespin or other toy with which he can pound. If you make a game of making "more noise than the thunder," he will not fear thunder, and may even think it fun.

Stimulate Feeling

1. Put him in a sitting position in his playpen. He may topple over, but he will practice balancing.

2. He will enjoy his bath. The water feels good and it is fun to splash.

3. In the bath, if he splashes water on his face, make a game of it by laughing. He will probably do it again and thus get used to water on his face.

4. Give him a cracker to eat by himself. If you show him the cracker and he opens his mouth, do not put it in his mouth; place it on the table. He will learn how to hold it and get it into his mouth.

5. Let him play with blocks that have finger holes. He will learn how these feel.

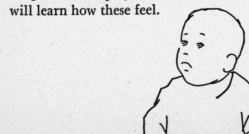

6. Put his hand on the radio or TV so that he can feel the vibrations as it plays.

7. In his playpen or on the floor, encourage his rolling from back to stomach. Show him a toy while he is lying on his back. Then put the toy on the floor beside him but out of his reach. If he does not roll over to get it, help him roll. He will soon learn to do it by himself.

8. Give him things of different textures to feel: cotton, sandpaper, sticky tape, terry cloth, silk, feather.

9. When outdoors, let him feel bricks, sidewalk, grass, leaves, dog fur, etc.

10. He will enjoy a small plastic pool outdoors in the summer when he can sit up well.

11. On a blanket outdoors, encourage him to roll over and over. Help him if he needs help. As he rolls, he will feel his whole body as it touches the ground.

Stimulate Generally

1. Let him play on the floor or in his playpen while you prepare meals in the kitchen.

2. Let him watch Daddy as he shaves.

3. Let him follow you around as you clean. These activities on the floor should be done for just a short while. He must learn to stay in his playpen too.

4. Put his crib or playpen near the window so that he can look out at whatever the scene affords.

5. Take him outdoors to play either on a blanket or in his playpen, or for a ride in his carriage.

6. Bounce him on your knee and sing to him.

7. Lift him in the air and lower him, but don't "throw" him. Do it again. Stop. See if he tries to restart the game by straining to be lifted.

8. Occasionally take him with you on visits to family and friends.

9. Let other people feed him and take care of him sometimes so that he gets used to others doing things for him.

Stimulate Imitation

1. When he bangs his fist or cup on his table, take the cup from him and imitate his rhythmic banging. Return the cup, and he will do it again. Keep playing this game, imitating all his movements; he will enjoy this repetition and learn to imitate yours in turn.

2. Wave bye-bye and see if he imitates you. If he does not, wave his hand for him.

3. Pat your hands together to play pat-a-cake. Until he learns, you might pat his hands together.

4. Sit him on your lap facing you. Put your forehead against his and say "Boom." Take your head away and do it again. Soon he will learn to move his head toward yours when you play this game.

5. See if he imitates smacking his lips in a kiss when you do.

6. Whistle and see if he will pucker up his lips and try too.

7. Squeeze a plastic squeeze toy and see if he does the same.

8. Play with other toys and see if he imitates your movements.

Spatial Relationships

The following activities are designed to help your baby learn about space. At this point he is just becoming aware of things in space, of himself in space, and of space itself.

1. Put a toy close to him for easy reach. Then move it farther away, so that he must make more effort to reach it.

2. Put two blocks on the table out of easy reach, one to his right and one to his left. He will learn to reach to either side of himself.

3. While holding him, put his bottle or toy on the table and turn both yourself and him away from it with your back to the table. See if he turns himself around to see it.

4. Hold him upside down for a moment so that he sees the world this way.

5. Hold him firmly around the middle, facing away from you. Whirl around gently.

6. When he plays on the floor, get down with him and crawl toward and away from him. He will experience nearness and distance. An older child can play this with him.

7. While sitting on the floor with him, let him throw down a block or other toy. Show him how to throw it, saying

"Down." Pick it up, saying "Up" and then give it to him. He will learn that there is a down and an up.

8. Give him space rings to explore. He can hold the outer ring and move the ones which are inside.

SAMPLE DAILY ACTIVITY PROGRAMS—Six to Eight Months

You could select activities for a daily program to include at least one activity from each category of training—seeing, hearing, feeling, general stimulation, imitation and spatial relationships. The baby's structured half-hour educational play period can consist mostly of activities for sitting at his table. For example, in DAILY PROGRAM II, below: The mirror, squeak toy, bouncing him on your knee, pat-a-cake, and blocks may be used for his half-hour structured play period. The other activities suggested for that day— radio, bath, etc.—can take place at any time during the day. You may wish to omit some of these activities if your baby is tired or if he does not like a particular one; you may want to include some activities from another chapter. In other words, the programs are intended to be flexible and, of course, pleasant for both of you.

Activities are listed briefly *in these examples of how you might put together a daily activity program for your baby. These same activities are often described in greater detail on the preceding pages, and there you will find, under the following categories, many more activities to choose from to give your baby's daily program variety and interest.*

Daily Program I

STIMULATE SEEING
√ Let him play with household items
√ Place floating toys in his bath

STIMULATE HEARING
√ Rustle tissue paper

STIMULATE FEELING
√ Practice sitting him in playpen
√ Let him play with finger-hole blocks

STIMULATE GENERALLY
√ Let him play nearby while you prepare meals
√ Let him watch Daddy shave

STIMULATE IMITATION
√ Imitate his banging and have him imitate you
√ Wave bye-bye

SPATIAL RELATIONSHIPS
√ Put a toy close to him and then farther away

Daily Program II

STIMULATE SEEING
√ Give him clothespin
√ Show him his image in mirror

STIMULATE HEARING
√ Give him plastic squeak toy
√ Play radio, phonograph

STIMULATE FEELING
√ Let him enjoy his bath
√ Play game of splashing water on him

STIMULATE GENERALLY
√ Put his crib near window
√ Bounce him on your knee and sing

STIMULATE IMITATION
√ Wave bye-bye
√ Play pat-a-cake

SPATIAL RELATIONSHIPS
√ Put two blocks out of easy reach, one to right and one to left
√ Turn him away from bottle or toy and see if he turns around to see it

Daily Program III

STIMULATE SEEING
√ Encourage his changing toy from one hand to other
√ Give him block in each hand and then give him a third block

STIMULATE HEARING
√ Give him bell on a handle
√ Hold bell behind him to right and then to left; see if he turns

STIMULATE FEELING
√ Put his hand on radio to feel vibrations
√ Give him different textures to feel

STIMULATE GENERALLY
√ Let him follow you around as you clean
√ Take him outdoors

STIMULATE IMITATION
√ Wave bye-bye
√ Play "Boom"

SPATIAL RELATIONSHIPS
√ Whirl around gently while holding him
√ Crawl toward and away from him

Daily Program IV

STIMULATE SEEING
√ Place "Baby-Activator" over crib
√ Drop small block on table; see if he will reach for it

STIMULATE HEARING
√ Call his attention to sounds of running water, footsteps, etc.
√ Rustle tissue paper, foil, etc.

STIMULATE FEELING
√ Encourage rolling on floor
√ Let him feel different textures

STIMULATE GENERALLY
√ Take him outdoors to play on blanket
√ Take him to visit friends

STIMULATE IMITATION
√ Smack your lips in a kiss
√ Play "Boom"

SPATIAL RELATIONSHIPS
√ Throw block "down"; pick "up"

Daily Program V

STIMULATE SEEING
√ Let him feed himself with fingers
√ Play Peek-a-boo

STIMULATE HEARING
√ Say "Bang, bang" when it thunders
√ Play radio or TV

STIMULATE FEELING
√ Let him feel bricks, sidewalk, etc.
√ Let him play with finger-hole blocks

STIMULATE GENERALLY
√ Whistle
√ Play pat-a-cake

SPATIAL RELATIONSHIPS
√ Give him space rings to explore
√ Hold him upside down for a moment

Daily Program VI

STIMULATE SEEING
√ Place cup upside down on his table
√ Teach him to turn bottle over to get object out

STIMULATE HEARING
√ Hold bell to right, to left, and behind him
√ Give him blocks with bells

STIMULATE FEELING
√ Let him play in water in plastic pool
√ Encourage him to roll over and over

STIMULATE GENERALLY
√ Let other people feed him

STIMULATE IMITATION
√ Play with toys; have him imitate

SPATIAL RELATIONSHIPS
√ Crawl toward and away from him
√ Whirl around gently while holding him

CHAPTER VIII | ACTIVITY PROGRAMS—
NINE TO ELEVEN
MONTHS

THE BABY can now roll over and sit up quite easily. Even though he can pull himself to a standing position when holding on to the sides of his crib, playpen or chair, he usually gets around by creeping on all fours. His hands are developing. By bringing his thumb and forefinger together he can pick up smaller things very neatly. He uses his forefinger to poke things and find out more about them. For example, he will put a finger into a cup or into any opening in a toy.

He is now more aware of what his family members are doing and he is able to imitate them in simple nursery games. He especially likes to play peek-a-boo. He is probably able to say "Mama," "Papa," "Dada," "Nana," but may not connect these words with their meaning yet. He also likes to try out various pitches in his voice, sometimes squeaking up high, sometimes making low sounds.

You can increase his regular play period to forty-five minutes or one hour a day. Be sure to let him play at some *one* activity for as long a time as possible, to stretch his attention span. He must still play alone at times so that he can entertain himself easily and learn things on his own.

Continue with those activities from the last chapter which he likes and which are still challenging. As in previous chapters, the following activities are grouped according to *what* you are teaching the baby and there will be some overlapping.

Stimulate Seeing

1. Let him finger-feed himself. He will now be able to do a pretty good job by using his thumb directly opposite his forefinger.

2. Help him fill his spoon and let him put it into his mouth by himself. He will lose a lot on the way to his mouth, but he will learn to do better as he works at it.

3. Put your hand over a cookie which is on the table. See if he lifts your hand to get the cookie.

4. Using a small toy, play the game, "Give it to Mommy." "Now, Johnny, take it" (call him by his name, and not "Baby"). He will enjoy giving it to you and taking it back and he will come to associate the words with the activity.

5. Put small toys into a larger container and take them out. Show him how, and he will do it over and over again.

6. Put little toys or spoons in a kitchen pot and put the lid over it. See if he picks up the lid and takes out the toys.

7. Choose a low kitchen cabinet and fix it up especially for him. Keep things in it that he may play with. Remove him from other cabinets when he gets into them and put him in front of his own cabinet. If he still goes back to the others, quietly remove him from the room and place him in his playpen. He will learn that he is not to go into the other cabinets. (Do not talk, scold or look angry; simply *teach* him that he may play in his cabinet only.)

8. Fling a toy ahead of him as he creeps. He will learn to do this by himself. Later use two toys for him to chase after.

9. Give him a large plastic ball when he is on the floor. He will push it easily and then creep after it.

10. Give him two or three small toys to hold in one hand.

11. Ask him, "Where's Mommy's ear?" "Where's Daddy's ear?" "Where's Doggie's ear?" Show him, and then see if he can show you.

12. Give him doughnut-shaped stacking toys. By poking his

finger through the hole, he learns that there is an inside and outside.

13. Give him a cup and a spoon. If he does not think of putting the spoon into the cup, show him how to do it. Letting go of an object in a small space takes practice. At first he may simply drop the spoon; then he may try to drop it into the cup and miss. Only later will he actually *put* the spoon into the cup.

14. Give him a cup and a one-inch block. He probably will hold one in each hand. Put the block into the cup if he does not. He will probably first learn to take a block *out* before putting it *in*.

15. Put a one-inch block on top of another (use wooden blocks—plastic is slippery and harder for him to work with). He will learn about stacking by first taking the top block *off* the bottom block. Do not be surprised if he can unbuild but not build. It may take some time before he actually puts one on top of the other.

16. Give him a crayon and sheet of paper. At first he will pound the crayon and try to taste it but not combine it with the paper. Show him how to scribble. If he doesn't understand, take them away and try again a few weeks later.

Stimulate Hearing

1. Play a record or the radio for him. He will probably bounce in rhythm to the music.

2. Let him beat on a toy drum. He will enjoy the motion and sound.

3. Give him a set of plastic disks on a chain. He will enjoy hearing the sound that they make, and will also like feeling them.

4. Let him listen to a clock tick. Say "Tick-tock," and shake your head in rhythm. He will learn to listen and shake his head in rhythm.

5. When outdoors, encourage him to listen to birds sing. When you hear a bird, point to it, saying, "bird."

6. Point to airplanes flying and try to imitate the sound with your voice when you hear one.

7. Teach him to follow simple directions, which he will enjoy: "Get Mommy's shoes"; "Get the teddy bear"; "Get the cookie." He may not understand the words at first, but if you show him, he will then do it later, when he does understand, without your showing him.

8. Ask him questions. He will first answer in gestures, and later by saying "Yes," or "No" to questions like "Are you wet?" "Bath?" "Nap?"

Stimulate Feeling

1. When outdoors, let him feel bricks, sidewalk, sand, grass, leaves or anything else he shows interest in.

2. When he is outside and the wind blows, blow on his hand so he can feel that kind of wind too. He himself may start blowing.

3. Let him crawl on linoleum, varnished wood floors, rug, tile, etc.

4. Give him empty boxes, jar lids, soap wrappers, cellophane, clean rags to play with.

5. Let him play with a "texture ball" (foam rubber stuffed into patchwork of many textured materials).

6. In his low kitchen cabinet place pots and pans, lids, other kitchen utensils, aluminum foil, tissue paper, wax paper, sandpaper, sticky tape for him to handle.

7. Dance to music while you hold him. He will enjoy the feeling of motion and rhythm.

Stimulate Generally

1. Include him in family activities so that he feels that he is part of the family. Let him participate in family fun.

2. Take him outdoors for carriage rides or put his playpen outdoors.

3. Take him with you to the supermarket.

4. Take him on visits and for a family meal in a restaurant.

5. Invite other children to play in your home. He will not actually play with them, but he will enjoy their presence.

Imitation and Speech

Long before the baby himself begins to speak, he understands you, more by your gestures and through the situation than through your words alone. If you say to him while he is, say, standing in the living room, "Open your mouth," he may very well not understand you. If you say the same words while he is in his high chair and you have a spoon in your hand, he will very likely understand. Your gestures and the situation act as clues to his understanding of your words. And it is through imitating your actions that he is eventually encouraged to imitate your speech as well. Using the words and sounds that go naturally with a game ("Here it is," "There it goes," "All gone," "Whee") also encourages him to speak. In first learning to talk, he will often use the same sound for several words—for example "ca-ca" might mean cookie, cake, cracker, and car. The following activities are suggested to encourage imitation of speech and movement:

1. Choose a sound that he already has made and say it yourself and laugh. He will laugh too and say the sound again. Repeat this several times.

2. Choose a simple sound which you have *not* heard him make before, laugh and see if he imitates the new sound.

3. Wave and say "Bye-bye."

4. Say "Hi" when someone comes into the house, and to him when you see him.

5. Using a toy phone, pick it up and say "Hi." Encourage him to imitate you.

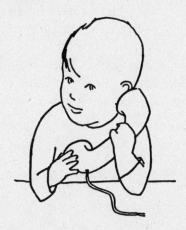

6. Play "Bouncy-bouncy" by bouncing him up and down as you sit, and he will imitate. Say the words; he will soon learn to bounce simply on hearing the words.

7. Sniff a flower.

8. Hit a toy with your hand.

9. Hit a toy with a stick.

10. Wave a toy in the air.

11. Pretend to drink from a toy cup; give him the cup.

12. Hold a block in each hand and hit them together.

13. Put some blocks in a container and shake it to make noise.

14. Show him how to make a doll's hands go pat-a-cake.

15. Play peek-a-boo. Show him how to hide.

16. Give him a toy phone and dial a number. See if he dials.

17. Show him how to make smacking noises and then kiss him on the cheek. Put your cheek against his mouth and see if he kisses you.

18. Play, "This little piggy went to market" with his toes. Let him have a turn pointing to your toes.

19. See if he imitates a coughing sound.

20. Breathe hard and make a panting sound for him to imitate.

21. See if he can imitate sounds like: *br-br, aboo, oh-oh, ghrr.*

22. Put your hand over your mouth and say *Wah, wah, wah,* Indian style.

23. Put your finger over your mouth and say *Sh.*

Spatial Relationships

1. While both of you sit on the floor facing each other, shake a small toy until his eyes are on it. Move it along the floor slowly until it is behind your back. See if he crawls around you to find it. Now place a briefcase or a large pillow between you. Again shake the toy until it holds his attention. Move it slowly across the floor until it is behind the pillow, out of his sight. See if he crawls around the pillow to find it. In another variation of this game, catch his attention with the toy and move it slowly across the floor until it is behind him, and see if he turns around to reach it.

2. Take a toy he likes and, as he watches you, drop it and kick it under a chair or low table. See if he goes to get it.

3. Let him creep through narrow and low spaces (between two chairs; between couch and wall; under a chair). He will learn how much space he takes.

4. Place him near a staircase and put a toy on the second step. He will try to get the toy, and in climbing to get it he will learn about space—up and down as well as depth. At first

he will be able to climb only one step but later he will be able to climb more.

5. Show him a familiar picture upside down. See if he will turn his head to see the picture upright. If he does not react, turn the picture upright, then hold it upside down again.

6. As you lift him and lower him say, "Up, down." This teaches the meaning of up and down, as well as the words themselves.

7. Show him how to put doughnut blocks on a spindle.

Self-awareness

The baby must learn about himself and have a mental picture of his own body and all its parts, and how the parts work to make a whole. The following activities are designed for this.

1. Put your baby in front of a mirror, either a full-length mirror or a smaller hand-held one, so he can observe his image.

2. Point to his eye, nose, mouth, etc. and say those words as you point. Say, "Where is your nose?" or "show me your nose." Teach him to point to his nose while he looks in the mirror.

3. Show him your eyes, nose mouth, and have him point to them.

4. Let him eat a cracker while looking at himself in the mirror. He will see his mouth, tongue, teeth, and will learn to point to these. He will also observe how he chews.

5. Hang a small lightweight bracelet of a material such as straw on one of his ears. He will reach for it. (In learning to distinguish, he may reach for the wrong ear.)

Cause and Effect

The baby is now learning that when he does something to a toy or other object with his hands, feet or body, something happens. We may say that he learns that he "causes" a certain "effect" to happen. For example, when he shakes the rattle it makes a sound. His *shaking* is the "cause" and the *sound* is the "effect." This is the beginning of logical thinking, and should be encouraged as you play with the baby. He will not understand words about cause and effect, but he will understand movement. Teach through movement.

1. Show him an alarm clock and how to push and pull the button to make the alarm go on and off.

2. Let him play with a device that reacts when he pulls a knob (a bell rings or a wooden block claps). He will continue to experiment with making the sounds.

3. Put a device on his crib or playpen which he can hit or kick to make it spin around.

4. Show him that when you wind a mechanical toy it moves. When it stops moving, see whether he gives it to you to wind or tries to wind it himself. If he gives it to you, show him again that winding makes it move. (Don't make long explanations; just show him.)

5. Any toy that moves or makes a sound by pulling a string, winding, or shaking can be used to teach him about cause and effect.

SAMPLE DAILY ACTIVITY PROGRAMS—Nine to Eleven Months

Activities are listed briefly *in these examples of how you might put together a daily activity program for your baby. These same activities are often described in greater detail on the preceding pages, and there you will find, under the following categories, many more activities to choose from*

to give your baby's daily program variety
and interest.
Stimulate Seeing, page 107
Stimulate Hearing, page 108
Stimulate Feeling, page 109
Stimulate Generally, page 110
Imitation and Speech, page 110
Spatial Relationships, page 112
Self-awareness, page 113
Cause and Effect, page 113

Daily Program I

STIMULATE SEEING
√ Let him finger-feed himself
√ Cover cookie with your hand; see if he lifts your hand to
get cookie

STIMULATE HEARING
√ Let him beat on a drum
√ Give him plastic disks

STIMULATE FEELING
√ Let him feel bricks, sand, grass, etc.

STIMULATE GENERALLY
√ Let him be around family activities
√ Take him to supermarket

SPATIAL RELATIONSHIPS
√ Have toy disappear behind your back

IMITATION AND SPEECH
√ Make one of his sounds and encourage him to imitate you

SELF-AWARENESS
√ Show him his image in mirror
√ Point to his eye, nose, etc., in mirror

CAUSE-EFFECT
√ Show him how to push alarm button on clock

Daily Program II

STIMULATE SEEING
√ Help him eat with spoon
√ Play "Give it to Mommy"

STIMULATE HEARING
√ Let him listen to clock tick
√ Call his attention to singing birds

STIMULATE FEELING
√ Let him crawl on linoleum, rug, etc.

STIMULATE GENERALLY
√ Take him for carriage ride
√ Invite other children to play

IMITATION AND SPEECH
√ Wave Bye-bye
√ Say "Hi"
√ Say "Hi" into toy phone

SPATIAL RELATIONSHIPS
√ Make toy disappear behind briefcase or pillow

SELF-AWARENESS
√ Show him your eyes, nose, mouth; have him point to them

CAUSE AND EFFECT
√ Let him play with a "baby activator"

Daily Program III

STIMULATE SEEING
√ Fling a toy ahead of him as he creeps
√ Give him two or three small toys to hold in one hand

STIMULATE HEARING
√ Call his attention to airplanes flying; make the sound with
  your voice
√ Let him listen to clock tick

STIMULATE FEELING
√ Give him empty boxes, jar lids, etc.

STIMULATE GENERALLY
√ Take him to supermarket

IMITATION AND SPEECH
√ Play "Bouncy-bouncy"
√ Sniff a flower
√ Hit a toy with your hand
√ Say "Hi" into toy phone

SPATIAL RELATIONSHIPS
√ Move toy until is disappears behind him

SELF-AWARENESS
√ Let him eat a cracker while looking in mirror

CAUSE AND EFFECT
√ Put a device on his crib that reacts to his touch

Daily Program IV

STIMULATE SEEING
√ Give him a large plastic ball to push on floor
√ Ask him, "Where's Mommy's eye?" etc. Show him how to
  point to it

STIMULATE HEARING
√ Give him directions for a simple task

STIMULATE FEELING
√ Blow on his hand when wind blows

STIMULATE GENERALLY
√ Let him be around family activities

IMITATION AND SPEECH
√ Hit a toy with your hand
√ Hit a toy with a stick
√ Play Bye-bye
√ Make a coughing sound

SPATIAL RELATIONSHIPS
√ Let him creep through narrow and low spaces
√ Lift and lower him, saying "Up" and "Down"

SELF-AWARENESS
√ Point to his eye, nose, etc.

CAUSE AND EFFECT
√ Show him how you wind a mechanical toy

Daily Program V

STIMULATE SEEING
√ Give him cup and one-inch block

STIMULATE HEARING
√ Ask him simple questions

STIMULATE FEELING
√ Place foil, paper, pots and pans in low cabinet

STIMULATE GENERALLY
√ Take him outdoors

IMITATION AND SPEECH
√ Wave a toy in the air
√ Pretend to drink from cup

SPATIAL RELATIONSHIPS
√ Place toy on step

SELF-AWARENESS
√ Hang a small lightweight bracelet on his ear

CAUSE AND EFFECT
√ Have him play with pull toy

Daily Program VI

STIMULATE SEEING
√ Place one one-inch block on top of another

STIMULATE HEARING
√ Give him directions for a simple task
√ Call him by name

STIMULATE FEELING
√ Dance while you hold him

STIMULATE GENERALLY
√ Let him be around family activities

IMITATION AND SPEECH
√ Show him to make doll's hands go pat-a-cake
√ Breathe hard and make panting sounds

SPATIAL RELATIONSHIPS
√ Show him how to put doughnut blocks on a spindle
√ Show him a familiar picture upside down

SELF-AWARENESS
√ Let him eat in front of a mirror

CAUSE AND EFFECT
√ Put a device on his crib that reacts to his touch

CHAPTER IX | # ACTIVITY PROGRAMS— TWELVE TO FOURTEEN MONTHS

THE ACTIVITIES of this chapter are appropriate for the baby who now sits without help, creeps on his hands and knees, pulls himself to a standing position and perhaps takes a step or two alone. He will not have fully achieved sturdy upright posture and firm walking. Although he probably will not eat well with a spoon, he will try. He will have better coordination in his fingers, enabling him to pick up small pieces of food and small toys with his forefinger and thumb.

He especially enjoys picking up and releasing small objects, particularly the latter, which is more difficult for him. For this reason, he repeats this activity again and again, practicing the act of releasing. He now likes more strenuous activities, pulling himself up, opening doors, being chased when he creeps, and hiding behind chairs to play "Where's baby?" He is becoming more sociable, playing with family members, laughing at unusual sounds or when others laugh. He will be able to imitate many things that members of the family do and will repeat a stunt when others laugh at him, putting on a show to keep himself the center of attention. Allow him to do this, show your appreciation and give him attention and plenty of love. Remember, though, he does not need *constant* attention. Let him be alone so that he does not grow up expecting attention at all times.

He probably will not yet be toilet-trained. However, you can put him on the potty if he has bowel movements at a regular hour and if he stays dry for two hours or awakens dry from a nap. He will toilet-train himself without being forced. All babies want to do what the older children or adults do— and using the potty is one way to follow suit.

He probably will be able to take his clothes off, especially if he has a soiled diaper. He can help in dressing by putting his arms into the armhole and holding his leg out for his pants, if Mother does not do it all for him.

Many parents wonder whether or not they should keep their baby in a playpen once he is able to creep, stand and cruise about while holding on to the furniture. An hour or an hour and a half's play with toys in the playpen will not harm his development, and it can give the parent freedom to get work done. He will still have time to move freely about the house when it is convenient for the parent. If the parent does not worry about harming him by keeping him in the playpen, he will stay in it happily.

About this time, parents become concerned about teaching their child what *not* to do or touch. The child who hears "No" very often soon learns to tune it out, or to use it to gain the parent's attention, or to show that he does not have to listen to the parent. At first the parent may think that he does not understand. Usually, if he ignores the "No," he does not *want* to understand. There is a better way of teaching him that some things are permitted and some are not. First, remove as much bric-à brac from his reach as possible to eliminate that constant "No." Then, if he does something you do not want him to do, simply say "No" once. If he does it again, remove him from the room, saying that only big boys (or girls) can play here. He may not understand all the words, but if you use them sparingly and show him by actions (removing him) what you mean, he will learn. It is very important that you do not show anger, or even feel anger, because he will then become angry at you, learning nothing from the situation itself. You must act quietly, firmly but pleasantly. He will then *learn* the rules of the home—things he can and cannot do. By setting up rules, following an orderly routine, and having some guidelines to follow, mothers do not get so angry at their children, nor do they feel nervous or emotionally upset. Instead, their knowledge of how to establish order and discipline gives them self-assurance and wins the cooperation of their children.

This chapter includes activities for language training and problem solving—baby is growing up! By now he should be able to work happily with you at his table for a full hour.

Activities may teach more than one skill, and will at times be listed in several categories. For example, teaching the child parts of the body can stimulate seeing, hearing, self-awareness and language. Such activities are listed under one or two categories, whichever are most important for that activity. In the case of parts of the body, these categories are "self-awareness" and "language."

Stimulate Seeing

1. Although he cannot eat with a spoon, he can use his fingers. Give him finger foods. By now, he can probably eat whatever the family eats and no longer needs baby food. Check with your doctor. When you feed him, give him his own spoon and show him how to use it. He probably will fill the spoon with his fingers, losing the food on the way to his mouth, but he is learning.

2. Let him help dress and undress. He will probably be able to take off his socks, put on a hat, and get one arm into a coat sleeve. Say "Push," as you put on his shoes, boots and mittens, and let him push.

3. He can help Daddy work, holding the screwdriver,

hammer or screws and handing them to his father as they are needed.

4. Play, "Where's baby?" Look for him when he hides behind a chair, table or sofa.

5. Roll a ball to him and let him roll it back to you as you both sit on the floor.

6. Play ball together. By now he will be able to throw, though unsteadily. He probably just waved it at you when you tried this at an earlier age, and couldn't let go.

7. He will enjoy playing with a truck that contains things to take out and put back.

8. Let him push a lightweight but rather large box ahead of him as he creeps on the floor.

9. Give him a marble and a marble track on an incline. He will learn to put it at the top and let it roll down.

10. Give him marbles to put into a box or other container. This is good practice in releasing objects into a definite and confined place. If he puts the marbles in his mouth, take them away from him. Do not give them back until he shows he has learned that they do not go into the mouth.

11. Give him large plastic beads with a bump on one end and a hole on the other (pop beads). He may not be strong enough to push them together, but perhaps he will be

able to pull them apart. Teach him how to line them up properly so that they can fit together; if he cannot push them together, help him.

12. Let him stack one-inch blocks. At first he may only be able to stack two together.

13. Show him how to make a train with the blocks by lining them up. Push them along saying, "Choo, choo, choo." Even though he has never heard or seen a steam engine and probably never will, he will love playing the game anyway.

14. Teach him to blow bubbles with a little wire frame or a soap-bubble kit. He will learn to catch the bubbles on the frame as they float in the air.

15. Make or buy a form board with three holes cut out— a circle, a square and a triangle. (There are some on the market with many pieces and many colors. However, for the beginner, these are too complicated. Also, the colors give him unnecessary help in matching without teaching him about the form.) Place the circle, square and triangle in front of him so that he can put them in the right holes. He may only be able to place the circle at first. Show him how to do the others, but do not work at it too long if he cannot see where they go. Try again later.

16. Let him play with a form box. This is a three-dimensional version of the form board, that is, a box with a lid with holes or various forms cut out. There are many kinds on the market, but choose the simplest and easiest to use. He may only be able to place the cylinders at first. Give him time; he will learn to do the others.

17. Make or buy large beanbags for stacking. For the beginner, these are easier to stack than large blocks.

18. Give him a small rubber ball and a ring. He will learn to push the ball through the ring.

19. He may be able to take graduated rings off of a stick but not to put them back on. Let him try to place them on the stick, even if he places them out of order. The idea of size takes a while to learn.

20. Let him put cereal bits into a small bottle. Give him something larger to try to put into the bottle (a piece of paper or a ball) so that he can learn that some things are too big to fit into the bottle.

21. At first, although he will know how to put cereal bits into the bottle, he will not understand that they can come out if he turns the bottle upside down. You can show him how to do this.

22. He will enjoy pouring water from a small pitcher or a cup into another cup while he is in his bath or outdoors.

23. Let him scribble with crayons on paper. Show him how to draw a vertical and then a horizontal line. He will imitate your line if you make it a game. Laugh and say *"Wheee!"* as you draw the line.

Stimulate Hearing

1. He will enjoy listening to the tick of clocks and watches.

2. Show him how to rock stiff-legged from foot to foot in time with the clock, saying "Tick-tock," as he rocks.

3. Give him rhythm instruments. Let him imitate your tapping faster-slower, louder-softer.

4. He can play a toy xylophone, singing as he plays.

5. Give him directions to follow: "Close the door," or "Get my shoes." (There are other hearing suggestions under Language Development.)

Stimulate Smelling

When you first tell him to smell something, he may not know what he should do. At first he will blow out air, but in time he will get the idea. Show him things that have a definite scent—flowers, bananas, apples, oranges, vinegar— and tell him "Smell it," as you place it under his nose. Show him how *you* smell it.

Stimulate Imitation

Do the following, and let him imitate you.

1. Scratch the surface of the table.
2. Drum your fingers on the table.
3. Open and close your fist.
4. Bend your index finger.
5. Open and close your mouth with a smacking sound.
6. Blink your eyes.
7. Touch your chin with your forefinger.
8. Wrinkle your nose.
9. Pull your earlobe.
10. Pat your cheek.
11. Strike the back of your hand with the other hand.
12. Tap your knees.
13. When you make the bed, let him help. He will imitate the way you pull the blankets and swat the pillows.
14. When you blow out candles, let him have a turn.

Imagination and Dramatic Play

Starting about this time, the baby will love to pretend. He will stir pots with a wooden spoon, taste and stir again. He may also pretend to eat foods he sees in pictures, and to treat his dolls or stuffed animals as if they were his babies. When other children come to play he may allow himself to be the "baby" in their play. Encourage him in this kind of play because he learns how to act like the people around him and he finds it fun.

Self-awareness

1. Ask him, "Where is my eye?" If he does not point to your eye, take his finger and put it near your eye, saying "Eye." Ask him again.
2. He may find it more difficult to show you his own eyes,

nose, mouth, teeth, hair because he is not able to see himself. Put his finger on his eye and say "Johnny's eye." Do the same with the other parts of his face. Then ask him, "Where is your eye?" or "Show me your nose."

3. Point to your eye and ask, "What is this?" When he is able to talk he will say "Eye." Do the same with the parts of a doll or puppet.

4. When looking at pictures in a book, ask him to find the dog's eye or the horse's eye. Then ask him, "Where is your eye?"

5. Let him see himself in a mirror. Ask him to show you his teeth. You might have him eat in front of the mirror so that he can see how he chews and uses his tongue and teeth.

6. He will enjoy seeing himself in the mirror when he wears a funny hat, new clothes or shoes.

7. If he sees his reflection in a mirror, a pot lid or some other shiny surface, ask him "Who is that?" If he does not answer, say, "That is Johnny."

8. Point to him and ask, "Who is this?" Teach him his name. Make a comparison by asking him, "Who is this?" when pointing to yourself.

Spatial Relationships

1. Give him a magazine with pictures upside down. See if he turns it right side up.

2. Show him a stuffed animal with its face toward him. When he starts to reach for it, quickly turn it around so that he sees the back of the animal. When he takes it, see if he turns it around to see the face.

3. Put three or four doughnut blocks on a stick. Turn the stack upside down and let the rings fall off. Let him try to put them back and turn the stick over again. He may be able to put them on the stick but not understand turning the stack over to remove the blocks. Do it again.

4. Give him some small toys inside a cup. He will probably take them out one at a time and then put them back into the cup. Show him that he can turn the whole cup over and that the toys will fall out all at once. Give him the toys in the cup again and see if he will then turn the cup over to get them out.

5. Play ball with him on the floor. Encourage him to move into a detour set-up which you have prepared in advance. Roll the ball under the sofa or other obstruction so that he cannot reach it except by detouring around. Tell him to get the ball. If he does not crawl around the detour, try this game again in a few weeks, when he may then be old enough to know what to do.

6. Place a cardboard vertically in front of him. Move a small toy slowly behind the cardboard and keep moving it until it shows up again at the other side of the cardboard. When you repeat this, see if he watches the second side of the cardboard ahead of time, anticipating your actions.

7. Show him how to hang clothes on hooks and towels on rods, teaching him about hanging things and about things going up and down.

Problem Solving

You can teach the baby to solve easy problems when you play with him. He will find this great fun and will learn an important lesson in careful watching, remembering and working out a solution to a problem.

1. Sit on a rug so that there is no sound to help him solve these problems. Hold out a toy that he likes very much. As he reaches for it, cover it so that a small part still shows. Use a white piece of cloth that he cannot see through. See if he can find the toy. Play the game several times.

NOTE: You must use something he really likes when you

play these problem-solving games or he will not bother to look for it. Some babies like a bright-colored necklace or string of beads. You can use boxes or thin pillows instead of cloths for hiding the toy.

2. Show him a toy and, as he reaches for it, cover the toy *and* his hand with the cloth. Let him find the toy. Try again.

3. Put a toy on the floor and, as he reaches for it, cover it completely with the cover, but do not cover his hand. Tell him to find the toy. Do it again.

4. Leave the white cloth on the floor on one side of him. Put another cloth of a different color (gray, for instance; you do not want to use a cloth with an exciting pattern so that he plays with it and does not play the game) on the other side of him. Now hide the toy under the gray cloth. See if he goes right to it **or** still tries the white one first. Do it again.

5. Hide the toy under the white, then under the gray, and again under the white cloth and see if he can go to the right one each time.

6. Now put a third cloth in front of him (a tan color will do) and hide the toy under each of them, in random order, from five to seven times. See if he goes to the right cloth each time.

7. Put a toy on the table so that he can reach it. As he looks at the toy, put your hand or a piece of cardboard between the toy and him. See if he pushes your hand out of the way or knocks down the cardboard to find the toy.

8. Show him a toy he likes and place it out of his reach on a flat pillow on his table. Place the pillow so that he can reach only one corner of it. Tell him to get the toy. If he is not able to get it, show him that he can pull the pillow toward him, which will then bring the toy near enough to reach. Do this several times. (Don't let him climb on the table to get the toy.)

9. When he can get the toy by pulling the pillow toward him, hold the toy about four inches above the pillow and see what he does. If he does not pull the pillow, but points, reaches, looks at or asks you for the toy, you can be pretty sure that he understands that pulling the pillow will not work now.

10. While he is sitting in a high chair, show him a toy he likes. Tie a string to it and slowly lower the toy to the floor. Put the end of the string across the tray of his chair near his hand. Tell him to get the toy. If he does not pull the string, show him how to do it.

11. While he is sitting at his table, show him a toy. Tie a string around it and put the toy on the table, but out of his reach. Stretch the string from the toy to his hand. Tell him to get the toy. If he does not pull the string to get the toy, show him how to do it. Try it several times.

LANGUAGE DEVELOPMENT

As the child learns language, living in the world becomes easier for him. He can ask for things he wants by name. For example, when he is very little, he can tell you that he wants water, by saying "Wah-wah." When he learns to say the word "cup," he will say it when he sees a cup. He is also learning the use of things. When asked, "What do you do with a cup?" he probably will be able to *show you* how he drinks (by pretending) before he is able to *say* "Drink."

With the help of language he can organize his world. He will learn that both cups and glasses are used for drinking, that they can hold milk or water, and later that they are "containers." He will also learn that containers hold things, and that other things are containers, too—a milk carton, Mama's handbag, a box.

Spoken language comes only after many experiences with things in many different situations. He will understand what you say to him long before he actually talks. Research has shown that babies who are reared in institutions with little human interaction are very slow in language development. Everyday living situations, play activities and family fun will help the baby to learn language.

Before he is ready to talk, you can show him what language is for. For example, when you teach him to point to things you name, he will soon get the idea that language is for pointing to things. Later, he will point to ask you for the name. Then you can give him names for things *he* wants to know. Still later he will learn that all of his actions can be expressed in words.

The following language activities are for the baby before he is able to talk.

1. Ask him to touch things. First teach him to touch parts of his own body. For example, hold his foot and say, "Foot." Then say, "Where is your foot?" If he does not touch his foot, put his hand on it. At this age, feeling the part of the body teaches him more easily than touching other things, such as a cup, spoon or ball. Do the same with hand, finger, arm, and so forth.

NOTE: In all of these activities, do not expect him to look in the direction of your pointing finger, especially if you are pointing to something in the distance. He will not understand, and will just look at your finger tip. Put your finger right on the object. Also, do not work at pointing activities too long or he will start to dislike the game. A little goes a long way.

2. Tell him to point to parts of the body by saying, "Where is your hand?" or, "Show me your hand." Show him how, by pointing to his hand with your finger. Then, taking the index finger of his right hand, show him how to point to his left hand. He can point with either hand; at this age children usually do not show preference for one hand or the other.

3. Ask him to point to *your* hand, foot, arm, and so forth, saying, "Point to Mama's foot," or "Where is Daddy's hand?"

4. It wil be easier for him to point to parts of your face than to parts of his own face without seeing it. Tell him, "Point to Mama's eye." Then put his finger near his own eye and say, "Johnny's eye." "Where is Johnny's eye?" "There's Johnny's eye," etc.

5. Show him items in the home and tell him their names slowly and one at a time. Ask him where each item is after you tell him. If he does not point, put his finger on the object and say its name. Keep trying and he will soon learn to point to an object.

6. Give him simple directions, such as "Get me a shoe," or "Give Daddy his paper," or "Put the spoon on the table." If he does not understand, show him how to do it. Be sure that you do these in play, showing him that you think it is fun.

7. Play a "Please and Thank you" game. Give him a small toy and then say "Please," as you put out your hand to show him you want it. When he gives it to you say, "Thank you."

Do it again; he will think this fun, and will later learn to use these words.

8. He will probably learn to shake his head meaning "No" quite early in life. Most babies learn this when they turn their heads away or from side to side to show that they do not want more food. They also quite often hear parents say "No" while shaking their heads.

9. Play "ring around the rosy" with him. When you say "All fall down," go down with him. Not only will he enjoy this but he probably will soon say "Down" as you go down.

10. You can use pictures to teach him language. Do not be surprised if he does not recognize pictures of the family or a picture of a dog in a book even though he has a dog. It takes a while for him to see the meaning in pictures. Show him a picture of a piece of fruit and then the fruit itself. Oranges, apples, bananas or any fruit he likes will do. At first just show him one piece of fruit and its picture. Paste the picture to a paper bag or to the bottom of a small pan and tell him, "Put the orange with its picture," or "In the bag." He will understand what to do if he must put it *into* something.

11. Show him how to look at pictures in magazines and books and how to turn pages. Name some of the things you see, and ask him to point to these. (Example: "There is the dog." "Where is the dog?" "Yes, there is the dog," putting his finger on the dog's picture.)

12. He will enjoy a book of animals and their babies. Show him both "dog," and "baby dog." (Don't say "puppy" yet; it may confuse him.)

Most children learn to talk before they are able to walk easily. From the end of the first year to the second birthday is usually the age of speech readiness. The baby should be given encouragement to speak at this time. You will be able to tell that he is ready to learn to speak when he tries to name things. It is interesting that all babies start with practically the same first words. Although the word for "mother" varies from language to language, the baby word in many languages as well as our own is "mama." Some words are easiest for all babies to say and are usually used to mean many different things. For example, "bah" or "baba" might mean bye-bye, baby, ball, or grandpa.

Encourage him to talk through the following activities:

13. If you first play games in which he imitates you in action or gesture, he will then try to imitate you in speech too.

14. Encourage babbling by imitating him. Laugh with him so that he sees that you think it is fun. Then *you* say a sound and see if he will imitate you.

15. At first, concentrate on words that he already understands, especially those with sounds that he has used in babbling. For example, if he says "baba" when he babbles, and you wave "bye-bye" when Father goes to work each day, he will imitate your action and probably begin to say "Ba-ba." He will then learn the meaning and say it at the proper time without your help.

16. It is helpful to use actions and words together as you teach him to speak. He will learn more easily because the meaning will be clearer. For example, show him a glass of water and let him drink it when you teach him "water." "Wah-wah" is all right for him in the beginning. He will say it properly when he has more experience in making sounds.

17. The easiest words will be those simple ones in which the same sound is repeated, such as "bye-bye," "ma-ma," "da-da," "na-na," "choo-choo," "wah-wah." These will probably be among the first words he learns.

18. Since he will be able to understand your actions and words before he can say them, use very simple language with

only a few words so that he will hear the important ones and learn them more easily. If it is bath time, simply say "Bath," and walk toward his bath and get it ready. Soon he will know what "bath" means and walk toward it when you say the word. Only later will he be able to say "Bath." Parents usually talk too much, which is why children do not bother to listen.

19. Teach him words that will be useful to him and not just to show off. Names of everyday items such as foods or things he uses or sees are better for him than a lot of silly cooing or long nursery rhymes.

SAMPLE DAILY ACTIVITY PROGRAMS—Twelve to Fourteen Months

From the following suggested plans, choose in such a way that you include daily at least one activity from each category of training. If you happen to be reading to him and he says he would like to play with a puzzle, you might suggest that he may play with a puzzle when you are finished with the story. It is best to plan the program and stay with it; if he does not wish to carry out an activity, simply shorten its time (do not stop completely) so that he will learn that it is necessary to complete a task.

Activities are listed briefly in these examples of how you might put together a daily activity program for your baby. These same activities are often described in greater detail on the preceding pages, and there you will find, under the following categories, many more activities to choose from to give

your baby's daily program variety and interest.
Stimulate Seeing, page 122
Stimulate Hearing, page 126
Stimulate Smelling, page 126
Stimulate Imitation, page 127
Imagination and Dramatic Play, page 127
Self-awareness, page 127 ·
Spatial Relationships, page 128
Problem Solving, page 129
Language Development, page 132

Daily Program I

STIMULATE SEEING
√ Let him feed himself with his fingers and start using spoon
√ Let him dress and undress himself

STIMULATE HEARING
√ Have him listen to clock or watch tick

STIMULATE SMELLING
√ Allow him to smell various things

STIMULATE IMITATION
√ Scratch surface of table
√ Drum your fingers on the table

IMAGINATION AND DRAMATIC PLAY
√ Show him how to pretend (he will do it all by himself pretty soon): stir pots, play house with others

SELF-AWARENESS
√ Ask him to point to your eye
√ Ask him to point to his own eye

SPATIAL RELATIONSHIPS
√ Give him a magazine upside down

PROBLEM SOLVING
√ Cover toy as he reaches for it
√ Cover toy and his hand as he reaches for toy

LANGUAGE
√ Ask him to touch things as you name them
√ Tell him to do something

Daily Program II

STIMULATE SEEING
√ Play "Where's baby?"
√ Roll a ball to him

STIMULATE HEARING
√ Rock stiff-legged to tick of clock

STIMULATE IMITATION
√ Open and close your fist
√ Bend your index finger

SELF-AWARENESS
√ When looking at picture of a dog ask him to point to the dog's eye. Then ask him to point to *his* eye

PROBLEM SOLVING
√ Cover toy on floor as he reaches for it
√ Hide toy under one of two cloths and let him find it

LANGUAGE
√ Tell him to do something
√ Play "Please and Thank you" game

Daily Program III

STIMULATE SEEING
√ Throw a ball to him
√ Put things into a truck and take them out

STIMULATE HEARING
√ Tap with rhythm instruments

STIMULATE IMITATION
√ Blink your eyes
√ Touch your chin with your finger

SELF-AWARENESS
√ Show his teeth while he looks in mirror

SPATIAL RELATIONSHIPS
√ Turn toy as he reaches for it
√ Put doughnut blocks on a stick

PROBLEM SOLVING
√ Alternate hiding toy under each of two cloths
√ Hide toy under each of three cloths

LANGUAGE
√ Play "Ring around the rosy"
√ Show him an object and a picture of the object pasted on a
    bag; have him place the object in its proper bag

Daily Program IV

STIMULATE SEEING
√ Let him help Daddy by handing him tools he asks for
√ Push a box in front of him as he creeps on floor

STIMULATE HEARING
√ Give him toy xylophone to play and sing along with

STIMULATE SMELLING
√ Play game of smelling various things

STIMULATE IMITATION
√ Open and close your mouth with a smacking sound
√ Blink your eyes

SELF-AWARENESS
√ Let him see himself in funny hat in mirror

SPATIAL RELATIONSHIPS
√ Empty toys from cup by turning cup over

PROBLEM SOLVING
√ Hide toy with your hand or cardboard
√ Pull pillow to get toy

LANGUAGE
√ Show him a book of animals and their babies

Daily Program V

STIMULATE SEEING
√ Roll a marble down an incline

STIMULATE HEARING
√ Give him directions to follow

STIMULATE IMITATION
√ Touch your chin with your forefinger
√ Wrinkle your nose

SELF-AWARENESS
√ Ask him "Who is that?" when he sees his reflection in mirror

SPATIAL RELATIONSHIPS
√ Hang things on hooks

PROBLEM SOLVING
√ Hold toy above pillow

LANGUAGE
√ Encourage babbling by imitating him
√ Teach him words with actions

Daily Program VI

STIMULATE SEEING
√ Push rubber ball through ring
√ Put cereal bits into small bottle

STIMULATE HEARING
√ Give him directions to follow
√ Rhythm instruments

STIMULATE IMITATION
√ Tap your knees
√ Blow out candles

IMAGINATION AND DRAMATIC PLAY
√ Pretend various activities with him

SELF-AWARENESS
√ Have him eat in front of mirror
√ Point to him and ask, "Who is this?"

SPATIAL RELATIONSHIPS
√ Put doughnut blocks on stick
√ Remove small toys from cup

PROBLEM SOLVING
√ Lower toy on string
√ Pull toy with string on table

LANGUAGE
√ Use actions along with simple words
√ Teach words which are useful

Activity Programs

TODDLING

TO RUNNING

CHAPTER X | ACTIVITY PROGRAMS—
FIFTEEN TO TWENTY
MONTHS

THE ACTIVITIES of this chapter are to be used
when the baby goes from creeping to toddling, and then
leaves toddling for running. This covers a longer span of
time than the previous chapters. The baby's growth is much
faster in the months immediately after birth. Although after
a year changes still occur from month to month, they are not
as significant or as dramatic from week to week.

Even by the time the baby is running, he has not yet
developed full upright posture. He walks with feet wide
apart and runs with stiff legs.

He is gaining more physical independence. He takes off his
own shoes, hat, mittens, and even unzips a zipper. Gross
motor activity, that is, use of his large muscles as in walking,
running and climbing, is more evident than fine motor activity—stacking blocks, picking up small things. He likes to
throw toys out of his playpen, partly because he can do it
well, now that his muscles are more developed. It is better to
leave the toys he throws out of his playpen than to pick them
up constantly and return them to him. He can practice
throwing balls or other small things when he can chase them
himself or when you play a game of catch with him.

Although he wants to feed himself, he still turns his spoon
over on its way to his mouth. Although he allows you to
feed him, he wants to hold his own spoon and put it into his

bowl occasionally. He can drink more neatly from his cup now, although he may take less milk during the day than when he had a bottle. Don't worry about this; gradually he will drink enough milk from the cup.

He probably will not listen to "No," but will demand his own way, even trying a temper tantrum. If you give in to him at such times, you only train him to have more tantrums. Instead, simply be unimpressed, walk into another room and busy yourself with something. Remember, do not get angry—you are trying to teach him that you are *not* impressed with such behavior; do not talk—just walk away. If he derives no satisfaction from his behavior (getting you angry can be a satisfaction) he will soon drop the behavior.

He will still sleep about twelve hours at night. At this age he may start bedtime routines to keep mother or father busy. It is wise to tell him (about ten minutes in advance) that it is now almost bedtime. You and he should put away his toys and get him ready. He should be washed and given his drink, put on the potty, diapered, told a short story, and then simply kissed and tucked in. If he calls to ask for more—water, toilet, kiss, or whatever—do not answer; he will understand that you are not going to continue to give him service. Allow him to sleep with the door either open or closed. If he becomes bothersome let him choose, explaining that his door can be left open only if he is quiet. Given the choice, young children usually prefer to have the door left open. It is all right if he talks to *himself* or sings until he falls asleep. If he awakens during the night, do not rush to him—give him a chance to go back to sleep. Do not play the game of quieting him down. He should sleep all night—but he will not, if he discovers this ability to awaken his parents for entertainment.

Some children may be toilet-trained by now. If the baby soils after being taken off the potty, keeping him on longer will not help. If he resists being put on the potty, do not force him. In other words, avoid toilet-training fights. Try putting him on the potty before and after meals and sleeping. He will train himself if *you* are not trying too hard to force him.

When you give him paper now, he will both scribble and imitate a line drawn with crayon. Toward the end of this period, his favorite words probably will be "oh, my," "all gone," "bye-bye," all of which are used when he completes something. At this age the baby is "into everything" if given the chance. You can still keep him in his playpen for a while either indoors or outdoors. Also he can be taught to play in his own room, staying there for as long as an hour. Put a gate up across the door at those times. At other times of the day he should have the run of the house and freedom to play outdoors. Your structured educational play period with him should be set at a special time of the day for about one hour.

In this chapter I no longer list separate sensory stimulation (seeing, hearing, feeling) because the child now experiences these mainly in combinations. His learnings are now quite complex.

Many of the following activities teach a variety of skills, although the activity may be listed under only one category. For example, "Time to take your bath" is included in this chapter under the teaching category of "time." Although stressing the concept of time, the lesson also teaches language and self-care, as well as sensory stimulation. It would be far too complex for parents to be concerned with all these incidental learnings. I suggest that you think only in terms of the category under which I have listed the skill. The incidental learnings come as a natural consequence of the activity itself.

Fine Motor Activity

1. Give him a set of plastic pop beads to put together and pull apart. Though he will probably understand that the bump goes into the hole, he may not have the strength to

join them. Starting with two beads, stand behind him, hold his hands as he holds the beads and say, "Push," as you help him. He will soon get the idea. Later you will have to hold only the end bead as he adds more. He may be able to pull them apart before putting them together.

2. Play dough and clay are good for teaching him to roll, pat, pinch, poke, make a pancake and anything else you or he can think of.

3. Small cars and trucks to push on the table or floor will help coordinate his legs, knees and hands.

4. A wagon with things to put in and take out is useful for pulling as well as for placing and removing things.

5. Give him small (one-inch) blocks for stacking and to use for making a train.

6. An activity box with many gadgets will busy him for a long time and teach him to use his fingers. You can make one to include locks, hooks and other pieces of hardware, or buy one.

7. Give him a toy telephone to dial and talk into.

8. Peg-and-hammer sets are excellent for learning the co-ordination required for hammering.

9. Give him a toy that reproduces animal sounds when the child pulls the string. He can say what he hears.

10. Books that have different types of material pasted into them, such as sandpaper, a feather, silk, etc., are excellent for feeling textures and for practice in turning pages. These can be either homemade or bought.

11. Show him how to stack several objects and then pick the whole stack up at the base to move them all together.

12. Books that have buttons to button, zippers to zip, etc., are commercially available and are good for teaching these tasks.

13. Let him start stringing beads. First use large beads and later small ones.

Gross Motor Activity

1. Most of his gross motor play will be natural activities: walking, running, climbing, carrying things. He should have time during the day to practice these indoors and outdoors.

2. A walker wagon steadies him as he learns to walk. Later he can use it to move blocks and toys from place to place. He may want to use his own stroller for such purposes.

3. Any toys that have a string for pulling or a handle for pushing or pulling are fine for him as he is walking.

4. Give him large blocks (made of foam rubber, cardboard or wood) to pile up or build with.

5. Encourage him to push rather heavy objects such as chairs or large boxes.

6. As he runs, he will enjoy both being chased and chasing you.

7. Play ball with him so that he can practice throwing the ball and running after it. Catching the ball will still be rather difficult for him.

8. Allow him to crawl under and between things to find "lost" toys.

9. In good weather he prefers to play outdoors. He can still play in his playpen for a while each day or in his own room with a gate stretched across the door.

10. While outdoors, let him play in water, a small plastic pool if possible. Give him containers of various sizes so that he can pour water from one to the other. He will not understand the size differences and may overfill the smaller one so that it spills. Be sure that he plays where spilling water is unimportant.

Self-awareness

1. Tell him to point to his foot, elbow, hand, and other body parts, and point to yours. Repeat this in front of a mirror. He should be learning more body parts as time goes on.

2. Give him a doll or a puppet, telling him to point to its body parts and then to his own.

3. Show him pictures of people and animals and ask him to name body parts.

4. Ask him what his name is or who he is, pointing to him. After telling him his name, ask him to say it. This may

take some practice. Use his nickname if this is easier for him to say.

5. Point to yourself and ask, "Who is this?" Tell him the answer and then ask *him* to repeat it. Point to him and ask, "Who is this?" See if he tells you his own name.

6. He will begin to get the idea that certain features come in pairs. When he is being bathed, ask, "Where is your knee?" and then, "Where is your *other* knee?" Do this with arms, legs, hands, eyes.

7. He may want to eat with the family to feel that he is a part of it. This should be allowed as much as possible. He should be given a spoon with which to practice, although he will do better with his fingers at this time.

Imitation

1. Show him pictures telling him to imitate the action. ("Yawn like the yawning bear," etc.)

2. When you set the table, let him help.

3. Let him help you dry the dishes.

4. Give him a small broom so that he can imitate your sweeping.

5. Smile, and he will too.

Imagination

1. Give him dolls and stuffed animals, pots, pans, play dishes and the like. He will pretend that he is taking care of his baby or eating with a friend.

2. Get down on the floor with him pretending that both of you are animals: dogs, horses, cats, cows. Walk on all fours, making the sound of the animal.

3. Let him pretend to drive when he is in the car with you.

Time

The newborn becomes frustrated when he wants a feeding or feels uncomfortable and must wait. This is probably his first lesson in time. Before he learns to speak, he will probably be able to wait without crying when Mother says, "Wait just a moment." He understands that those words mean "Mother will do it *soon*."

You can more easily teach the baby about time if you run your home on some orderly basis. The baby will soon learn "Time to get up," "Time for breakfast," "Time for play," "Time for nap," "Time for Daddy to come home." As each day goes along similarly to the last, he begins to *feel* a sense of the passing of time. This is not to say that you must be rigid and never do something at a different time or in a different way; it only means that there should be an overall order in the home. If you have been keeping the baby on a schedule and have been working with him at a special time of the day he probably knows the "right" time for his activities and goes to the work table all by himself. He is developing a "built-in clock."

1. Start using the words "after" and "before," so that he learns about the past, present and future. "After you drink your milk you may have the cookie"; "Before we go for a ride in the carriage, you must take a nap"; "Now we can go out."

2. When he asks for something and you are busy you can say, "Just a minute," or "In a moment." He will begin to learn time words—and to wait.

3. Mention times to him: "Time to eat"; "Time to take your bath"; "It is eight o'clock and time to go to bed."

Problem Solving

Sit on a rug so there will be no sound to help him solve these problems.

1. Put a white, a gray, and a tan cloth in front of him, leaving some space between them. Hold a toy in your hand so that he can still see a small part of it and move your hand along a path under each cloth. He should see your hand between each cloth as it moves along. Leave the toy under the last cloth. See if he looks under the last cloth. Do this several times, leaving the toy under a different cloth each time.

2. Place a toy in front of him and cover it with the white cloth, then with the gray, and finally with the tan. Overlap the cloths in such a way that he cannot take them all off at one time. Watch him as he takes off the top cloth, finding not the toy but another cloth. See if he works until he finds the toy.

3. Put a small toy in your hand while he watches you and then put your hand under an opaque white cloth. Leave the toy under the cloth, take your hand out and show him your closed fist. If he does not open your hand, show him that the toy is no longer in your hand. See if he looks under the cloth for the toy. Do this several times.

4. Put the gray cloth next to the white one. Let him see the toy in your hand and put your hand under the gray cloth, leaving the toy. Show him your hand. See if he looks in your hand and then under the gray cloth. Do this several times.

5. Hide the toy in your hand and then under either the gray or the white cloth, alternating between them—about five times. See if he looks under the right cloth.

6. Leave the white and gray cloths in front of him and add a tan one. Hide the toy in your hand and then, in mixed order, about five to seven times, under the cloths. See if he looks under the right cloth each time.

7. Hide a toy in your hand so that it does not show and move your hand along a path under each cloth. Leave the toy under the last cloth. Do this several times from left to right and then from right to left so that the last cloth becomes the first cloth. Leave the toy under the last cloth each time.

8. Put the toy in your hand and move your hand along a path under the three cloths, but this time leave the toy under the first cloth. See if he looks under the first cloth or if he looks under the last cloth (as he's been accustomed to doing), then under the next to the last, and finally under the first cloth.

9. Show him a toy as he sits in his chair. Place the toy on the table out of his reach and place a stick, long enough to reach behind the toy, near his hand. Tell him to get the toy. If he does not know what to do, demonstrate the use of the stick to get the toy, pushing it closer to him and away from him several times. Try the whole game again and see if he has learned what to do to get the toy.

10. As he sits on a high chair drawn up to a large table, put two flat pillows or pads out of his reach. Tie strings to each pad and draw the strings from the pads to his hands. Show him a toy that he likes and place it on one of the pads. Tell him to get the toy. If he does not pull the right string, show him how to do it.

11. Using the same setup, put the toy in the space between the two pads and see if he realizes that pulling the string will not bring him the toy.

12. Place a toy in a small lidded box and close the lid; put the closed box into a second, larger box and close the lid. Tell him to find the toy. Do this several times.

13. Put a small empty box with closed lid into a larger box; close the lid. Give it to him and see if he remembers that there is no toy in the boxes now. Whether he remembers or not, he can take the boxes apart.

14. Put a toy in a small box and close the lid. Put the closed box into another box and then into a third box which is still larger and place the lid on it. Tell him to find the toy.

15. Play the game with three boxes, but without putting a toy inside. See if he remembers that you did not put a toy in the smallest box.

16. Make a cylinder by drilling a tunnel about one and one half inches in diameter through a block of wood about five by twelve inches. Put a toy into one end and push it through with a stick (about twenty-four by one quarter inches). Tell him to watch for the toy at the other end. Show him how to do it again, then put the toy in one end of the "tunnel" and put the stick next to it. Tell him to get the toy with the stick.

17. Show him how a set of three nested cups fit into each other. Place all the cups in front of him and see if he can put one into the other correctly. This may take some practice; it is easier if the cups fit together easily. If you have a set with six cups, give him the very largest, the smallest, and the one in the middle to start with.

18. Put a small piece of candy or cereal into a plastic bottle two inches high by one inch wide. The bottle opening must be small enough so that he can not get the candy by putting his fingers into it. See if he can turn it over to get the candy. If he does not, show him how to do it.

19. Place a long necklace (fifteen inches of small linked chain will do) stretched end to end and a plastic cup in front of him. See if he will try to put the necklace into the cup. If he does not do it, take them away and put the necklace into the cup behind your back and then give it to him so that he sees the necklace inside the cup. Take the necklace out of the cup and give both of them to him again. See if he tries to put the necklace into the cup. If he cannot do it, show him how to bunch it up first, or dangle it in, or roll it up and then place it into the cup.

20. He will be able to place some of the forms into a form box. The cylinder and cube are the easiest to place. (This toy can be used again in the future, as he learns to put all the forms into the proper slots.)

21. He will probably be able to put together three-piece and later four-piece puzzles. You can help him at first. Tell him, "Turn the piece around," or "Try the other piece," but do not do it for him. You might have to show him how to do it several times until he learns.

22. Put a red sock on his foot. Show him a red and a yellow sock and say, "Which one goes with the one on your foot?" He will learn to match colors. Do the same with red and blue, blue and yellow. As he selects the color, mention the name of the color.

Language

The baby will still be able to understand more language than he can speak. Parents should keep their language quite simple so that he will hear what is most important and thus learn new words more easily. Parents can serve as a dictionary for the baby. When he wants to know the word for something, you can tell him the name and give a simple definition of use. For example, if he sees the dog drink from his bowl and says, "Cup," you can say, "No, Johnny drinks from a cup. This is a bowl. The dog gets a drink in a bowl." Say, "What do you call this?" "Yes, a bowl." He may not remember, and then you simply tell him the word again. He will soon learn it. You can also give him the word for those actions that he now notices. For example, when he watches you make toast and he says, "Toast" as it pops up in the toaster, you can say, "Yes, toast pops up."

While the baby is learning his basic vocabulary, you can teach him some words that might be called "baby talk" ("mama," "choo-choo," "ta-to," (for potato), "wah-wah," for water, and the like). Babies learn to say "mama" before they can say mother, "dada" before father, "nana" before grandmother. Research on babies' speech development shows that children of parents who play speech games like those in this book (using words that are not the real words but are easy for children) are, by thirty months of age, saying these words properly; in fact these children actually know more other words than children who have not had this kind of teaching. (Warning: If parents talk baby talk for years, children will be late in learning to talk correctly.) These easier versions should be used only when the baby is just beginning to use words; they should not be used beyond the time he can say the proper word—about two and a half years old for most children, for others a little younger or a little older. Actually, it will surprise you to find how quickly he learns complicated words once he really starts combining words into phrases and sentences. Since the baby will be able to understand more language than he can express, you can help him learn language by naming words in play activities with toys, with other objects and with pictures, even if he does not talk much.

1. To teach him the relationship between pictures and words, cut pictures of ordinary things from magazines. Show him the real object and its corresponding picture and, naming the object, tell him to put them together. The pictures you choose should be very clear and as much like the object as possible. Look for pictures of a spoon, a cup, a toothbrush, soap, foods. Sometimes the box or wrapper in which it is

bought has a picture you can use. It is helpful to put the picture in a box or pan or to paste it on a paper bag, because he will understand more easily if you ask him to put the spoon, for example, into the box that has the matching picture. Tell him, "Put the soap into its box (or bag)." You can then let him pretend to wash his hands with the soap. If these games seem too difficult or if he does not appear to like them, stop and try again in a few weeks. Don't force him.

2. Give him *one* object and *two* pictures so that he has to choose the right picture. For example, give him a banana and a bag with a picture of a banana and a bag with a picture of an orange. Tell him, "Put the banana in its bag." When he is able to do this, give him one object and three pictures.

3. Give him *two* objects and *two* pictures—a banana and an apple, and pictures of each one. Tell him, "Put the banana in its bag"; after he does that, say, "Now, put the apple in its bag." Try later with three objects and three pictures.

4. To encourage him to talk, start a scrapbook for him. Cut pictures of simple objects from magazines. Ask him their names. If he says the name, give him the picture to paste in his scrapbook. You will have to help him with the pasting, but do not do it for him. *If he is still unable to talk,* show him two pictures and ask him to point to the one you name. (For example, show him a picture of a car and a chair and say, "Show me the car." If he points to the car, give him the car picture to paste in his book. If he does not point to the car, do *not* give him the picture. The object is to teach him the word, and not simply to paste.) If he is unable to either name the object or to point to the correct picture, he is not ready for this game; stop and try again at a later date.

5. Show him pictures cut from magazines, or pictures in books and magazines and ask, "What is this?" or "What do you call this?" Tell him the name if he does not know it, but first give him a little time to think of it

6. Give him directions to follow. "Feed your doll, she's hungry." "Bring Mama her shoes." Be sure to make it a game.

7. Tell him to point to parts of the body: head, nose, eyes, hair, mouth, neck, knees, arms, feet, toes, fingers, nails, belly-button. He will be able to point to more parts than he can name.

8. During his bath say, "Wash your hand," "Wash your *other* hand" (knee, other knee). Keep it fun.

9. Give him simple words to describe what happens to things. For example, if he sees a dog running, say, "Dog runs." When the dog has gone away say "Dog all gone." He will learn to say these.

10. Show him there are words for all his actions and for yours. "Johnny is throwing the ball." "Mama is cooking dinner." "Daddy is hammering nails." "You are playing with your doll." "You are tearing paper."

11. When he points to something, as if asking what it is, give him the word he wants to know.

12. Show him that talking is used for expressing moods and feelings. You can do this by using different inflections and differing degrees of loudness and softness.

13. When eating he will understand "More," "No more," and "All gone," and will probably learn to say them soon.

14. He can begin to learn different words for people. At first he may have said "Mama" when he saw any lady or "Daddy" for a man; you can now teach him, "lady," "man," "boy," "girl."

15. Once he starts to talk, he may not always remember a word that he knew the day before. Just tell it to him if he points and he will then say it. Do not be surprised to hear him still use jargon.

16. When you read a story to him many times, he will probably memorize it, and he will let you know if you skip a page

17. Teach him the words used for counting. He will not know how to count, but he will like the sound of "One, two, three." Add more numbers as he can remember them.

SAMPLE DAILY ACTIVITY PROGRAMS—Fifteen to Twenty Months

Select activities from every category for each day of training.

Activities are listed briefly in these examples of how you might put together a daily activity program for your baby. These same activities are often described in greater detail on the preceding pages, and there you will find, under the following categories, many more activities to choose from to give your baby's daily program variety and interest.
Fine Motor Activity, page 147
Gross Motor Activity, page 150
Self-awareness, page 151
Imitation, page 152
Imagination, page 152
Time, page 153
Problem Solving, page 154
Language, page 158

Daily Program I

FINE MOTOR ACTIVITY
√ Pop beads
√ Small cars to push

GROSS MOTOR ACTIVITY
√ Walker wagon
√ Pull toy

SELF-AWARENESS
√ Point to body parts

IMAGINATION
√ Doll play

TIME
√ "Before" and "after"

PROBLEM SOLVING
√ Leave toy under one of three cloths
√ Cover toy with three cloths
√ Turn bottle to get candy out

LANGUAGE
√ Object and picture
√ Two objects and two pictures
√ Use action words

Daily Program II

FINE MOTOR ACTIVITY
√ Pop beads
√ Play dough
√ Wagon (put in and take out)

GROSS MOTOR ACTIVITY
√ Large blocks
√ Play outdoors

SELF-AWARENESS
√ Point to body parts on puppet and then on self

IMITATION
√ Imitate action in pictures

TIME
√ "Before" and "after"
√ "Time to eat"; "time for ———"

PROBLEM SOLVING
√ Hide toy in your hand (one cloth)
√ Hide toy in your hand (two cloths)
√ Hide toy in your hand (three cloths)

LANGUAGE
√ Scrap book
√ Name pictures
√ Give him directions to follow

Daily Program III

FINE MOTOR ACTIVITY
√ Activity box
√ Toy telephone

GROSS MOTOR ACTIVITY
√ Play indoors and outdoors
√ Chase him

SELF-AWARENESS
√ Point to body parts
√ Point to yourself and to him

IMITATION
√ Set the table

IMAGINATION
√ Pretend you are an animal

TIME
√ "Just a minute"

PROBLEM SOLVING
√ Move toy in your hand under three cloths
√ Reach toy with stick

LANGUAGE
√ Scrap book
√ Give him directions to follow
√ Describe actions
√ "More"; "No more"

Daily Program IV

FINE MOTOR ACTIVITY
√ Animal talk toy
√ "Touch-me" book

GROSS MOTOR ACTIVITY
√ Play ball

SELF-AWARENESS
√ "Where is your knee?" "Other knee?"

IMITATION
√ Imitate action in pictures

IMAGINATION
√ Pretend he is driving car

TIME
√ "Time to ———"

PROBLEM SOLVING
√ Put toy on pad with string
√ Put toy between two pads

LANGUAGE
√ Give him the word he wants to know when he points to something
√ "Mama"; "lady"; "girl"
√ "One, two, three"

Daily Program V

FINE MOTOR ACTIVITY
√ "All by himself" book

√ String beads

GROSS MOTOR ACTIVITY
√ Crawl under and between things
√ Large blocks

SELF-AWARENESS
√ Point to body parts
√ Eat with family to be part of family

IMITATION
√ Imitate action in pictures
√ Dry dishes together

IMAGINATION
√ Pretend you are an animal

TIME
√ "Time to ———"
√ "In a moment"

PROBLEM SOLVING
√ "Push through"
√ Form box

LANGUAGE
√ Read a story to him
√ Count
√ Tell him action words

Daily Program VI

FINE MOTOR ACTIVITY
√ Pop beads
√ Small blocks to stack
√ Peg and hammer set

GROSS MOTOR ACTIVITY
√ Water play
√ Chase him

SELF-AWARENESS
√ Name body parts

IMITATION
√ Give him small broom to imitate sweeping

IMAGINATION
√ Doll play

TIME
√ "Before" and "after"

PROBLEM SOLVING
√ Put toy in box and all into a larger box
√ Close box without toy and place in large box

LANGUAGE
√ Scrap book
√ Name pictures
√ Action words

CHAPTER XI | ACTIVITY PROGRAMS—
TWENTY-ONE TO
TWENTY-NINE MONTHS

THE CHILD is now less of an infant and more of a child. He can run better without falling, but he does not turn sharp corners or slow down very easily. He can partially dress and undress himself, but he may, for example, get both legs in one pant leg. He can put two or three words together in a phrase or sentence. His fine motor coordination is fairly well developed so that in feeding himself he does not turn his spoon over on its way to his mouth. He probably likes to push his own baby carriage, stroller, or wagon, and he likes to climb; especially, he enjoys rough and tumble play with his father.

If his bowel movements are regular and occur after meals he may be trained to go to the toilet once or twice a day for these. He may do better if you allow him to go to the toilet by himself. He probably can keep dry for one and one-half to two hours, and he may often ask to go to the toilet during the day; however, he is still likely to be wet when you get him up in the morning. Some authorities suggest awakening the child and putting him on the toilet at about 10 P.M., but others believe he should sleep throughout the night without being disturbed, pointing out that he will learn to keep dry as he gets older and has more control. I prefer the latter course. Children who do urinate when aroused by their parents are usually almost asleep and therefore unaware of what they are doing; others simply get angry when awakened, which does not accomplish the training but in fact causes conflict between parent and child over an issue that should be as free of conflict as possible. It is best, then, not to expect your child to stay dry all night at this age. As he gets older, develops control, and takes responsibility for toileting and for the other aspects of his life, he will stay dry at night.

Some children get fussy about choosing foods to eat. Whether he is fussy or not, continue giving your child small portions of a balanced meal and add seconds of those foods that he asks for. He may eat better at lunch or breakfast if he is left to himself at his table. If the family eats dinner together, allow him to join the group. If he disturbs the meal, quietly remove him from the table. He will behave properly at the next meal. Remember, he will eat well if you do not worry about his intake of food.

Although he probably plays by himself when other children are around, he really enjoys their presence. Children of this age often engage in "parallel play," that is, being in the same room, but not seeming to pay much attention to each other. This is the beginning of real interaction, which will come later on. He should have a solitary play time as well during the day. A gate on the door to his room can still be used. He will enjoy some active play with an adult, building a good relationship with him. However, his hour of structured educational play should now be mostly at his table, where he is learning to sit and work for longer periods of time. The active play might take place at another time of the day for ten to fifteen minutes, or longer if you have the time.

Fine Motor Activity
1. He is interested in mechanical things with on-and-off switches. Let him turn on the lights, open doors by turning doorknobs, turn on the faucet when washing hands, and play

with a few wind-up toys. (Wind-up toys teach cause-effect relationships and fine motor activity, but do not let him play with these at the expense of other toys with which he has to work harder and be more involved.)

2. Give him beads to string. When he masters the larger beads, give him smaller ones.

3. Small pegs that fit into pegboards are excellent for fine motor development.

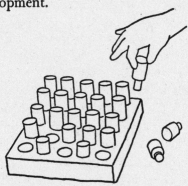

4. He will be able to stack blocks higher, now that he has better control of letting go of objects. See how many one-inch blocks he can build up. He may still enjoy making a train of the blocks.

5. A toy with screws and wooden screwdriver and small jars with screw caps will please him and help him to develop hand skills.

6. Jigsaw puzzles assist in fine motor development. Do not discourage him by offering puzzles with too many pieces. Judge his ability; after he is able to do a puzzle with three pieces, then try one with four, and so forth.

7. Drawing with crayons, pencil, chalk, and painting with water colors and brush or finger paints are fun and good for fine coordination.

Gross Motor Activity

1. Allow your baby the freedom to run, romp and climb, indoors and outdoors. It is a good idea to set limits in the home; for example, if you do not wish to have him climb on tables, cabinets or certain chairs, be specific—let him know what he may do and what he may not do. If he does not follow the rules, remove him from the "adult" room and tell him that he is not yet old enough to play properly in that room. Quietly pick him up and put him into his own room with the gate on the door. Look pleasant and do not get angry or talk too much; just remember that you are teaching him to behave within the rules of the home.

2. Play ball with him. He will now be able to throw the ball more easily.

3. Show him how to play "hide and seek." Tell him to hide behind a piece of furniture and then ask, "Where is Johnny?" "Oh, there he is." It will be more difficult for him to understand what he should do when *you* hide from him. You might try to show him by including an older child in your play whom you help to "find."

4. He will enjoy pulling his wagon and giving a ride to his dolls or stuffed animals.

5. Show him how to do a somersault by rolling him over. Let him try by himself.

6. Show him how to walk on tiptoe.

7. He may be ready to attempt standing on one foot; this balancing is rather hard, but he can try.

8. He will especially enjoy roughhouse with either father or mother.

9. Play "ring around the rosie" and "London Bridge is falling down."

10. Allow him to use a box, step stool or special chair to climb on to get something he wants. By climbing he will begin to understand about heights. (Remember, if you do not want him to climb on some one item, make this clear to him. Again, remove him from the room quietly, and put him in his own room, so that he can learn the rules of the home.)

11. A toy on which he can sit and ride by pushing himself is fun and good for using his legs.

Smelling Activity

He will learn more about the world by smelling things. Put each of the following in small jars: cinnamon, vanilla, chocolate, pepper, garlic powder, vinegar and any other items with strong odors. Tell him to smell the bottle after you open it. Ask him if he likes it or not. You can tell him the name of what he is smelling, but do *not* expect him to tell you the name when he smells a jar. It takes long experience to name the different odors.

Self-awareness

1. Place his hand or foot on paper. Draw an outline of his hand or foot with crayon or felt-tipped pen. Show him the "picture" so that he can see the shape.

2. Have him lie down on a large piece of shelf paper. Trace an outline of his body. Tape the picture on a wall and let him color it with crayons to match the color of his clothing.

3. Make the head, body, arms and legs of a human figure out of clay or play dough. Let him help you put the pieces together to make a man. As you work, explain to him that the arm goes on at the top of the body and let him look in a mirror and also feel his own arm and shoulder. Do the same when attaching the legs.

4. Make a doll out of felt or flannel and put it on a felt or flannel board. Cut out eyes, nose, and mouth, and tell him to find his own eyes, nose, and mouth.

5. Cut a large picture of a human figure from a magazine and paste it on cardboard. Cut it into the major body parts, making a jigsaw puzzle. Let him put the pieces of the man together. (Puzzles of the human figure are also commercially available.)

Imagination

Until now the baby has been learning about himself and how he fits into his world. As he recognized himself in a mirror, named his body parts and compared them with yours, he made himself the center of attention as he was developing his self-awareness. He will still be learning about himself, but now objects will be the center of his attention and the basis for his imagination as he develops awareness of the world, other people, and objects. He will cuddle and hug his doll or stuffed animal as you do him. He will try to feed them, and he will sound very funny to you when he scolds them using some of your words and inflections. Any toy or object that lends itself to imaginative play is fun and leads to creative activity.

Time

1. Continue to teach him about time by reminding him frequently, "Time for breakfast," "Time for nap," "Time for school" (your teaching-playtime at his table).

2. Use the words "before," "after," "now," "first," "last."

3. He will begin to understand when you say "Yesterday," "Today," "Tomorrow."

4. Although he will usually use present-tense verbs: "I *do* it now," "I *go* now," past-tense verbs will start to have meaning for him: "We *went*"; "We *did* it yesterday."

5. Future tense can also be used: "We *shall go*"; "We *shall do* it."

6. Words telling faster and slower passing of time can be used: "hurry," "slowly," "slower," "faster," "in a while," "wait."

Weight

Give him various things to lift so that he can feel their weight: feather, rock, beanbag, paperweight, piece of iron. milkweed seeds, small box with light or heavy objects in it (small raisin box with either raisins, tissue paper, pebbles, or heavy metal).

Self-care

1. Dressing lessons are important. Usually the child who is learning to dress himself takes a long time to do so when parents are in a hurry. Parents then feel that it is easier to dress the child than to wait so long for him to dress himself. One of the goals of this book is to help you teach your child to become independent at an early age. Teaching the child to dress himself should not be done when you are in a hurry. Choose a time of the day to practice putting on clothes when there is time for a lesson. You might want to do this instead of your usual lesson plan or you might do this as an extra lesson during the day.

2. Again, washing lessons should be given to the child when he is not in a hurry to get ready for an event. The bath, if you allow time, may be used to let the child learn to wash himself. He should also be given practice in washing hands and face at the sink.

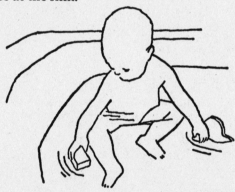

3. Tooth-brushing lessons may be given to the child at a time when you have time to teach him the correct way to brush his teeth. He should learn to brush his teeth.

4. A child who does not respond to the request to come to the table with clean hands should not be given his meal

until his hands are washed. Many families have solved the dressing problems of their young children by not offering breakfast until the child is dressed. If the child dawdles and other family members are finished with their breakfast by the time the child is dressed, Mother has the food put away and does not give him his breakfast. He will hurry up and dress very fast the next morning (unless Mother "feels sorry" for him and gives him cookies after the breakfast hour because he is hungry). It is important to have this situation become a "logical consequence" of dawdling and not a punishment inflicted by Mother. The logical consequence teaches the child an important lesson and is done without adult anger. Punishment only creates anger in both parent and child, and little teaching results.

Problem Solving

1. Have him arrange plastic rings, graduated in size, on a stick, from largest to smallest. Start with only three rings and when he can do those in order, give him several others, one at a time, until he is able to place all of them on the stick from largest to smallest.

2. Teach him "big" and "little." Cut two circles out of cardboard, one twice the size of the other, and put them on his table. Cut another two circles of the same size and give them to him. Tell him "Put the big one with the big one and the little one with the little one." (All four circles should be the same color so that this task is not confused with matching colors.)

3. Put one big and one little circle on the table and tell him: "Give me the big one." "Give me the little one."

4. If he can talk, put the circles on the table, point to one and ask, "Which one is this, the big one, or the little one?"

5. Give him three nested cups to put together. He will learn to put them together in order.

6. Put three or four poker chips or buttons on a three-by-five card, making a design. Give him the same number of chips or buttons and a card and have him copy your design. Make another design and tell him to copy that one.

7. He should be given simple jigsaw puzzles to put together. Start with three-piece, then four-piece puzzles.

8. He will probably now be able to place all the forms into the top of the form box. Give him time to practice this task.

9. You can begin to teach him about counting. He will first have to learn the difference between "one" and "many." Put bits of cereal on his table. Show him "one." Tell him, "Give me one." Show him that lots of pieces are "many." Then say, "Give me many."

10. Put two cups on the table, one in front of him and one in front of you. Show him how to play "One for me, and one for you." Put one cereal bit into his cup, then one in yours.

11. Put a red cardboard (two by two inches) and a similar blue cardboard on the table. (Use bright shades of red and blue.) Give him a duplicate red one and say, "Put this with the one just like it." If he cannot do it, show him that it goes with the red one and say, "Red."

12. Put a red and a blue cardboard on the table. Say, "Give me the red one," then, "Give me the blue one." Do the same with red and yellow and with yellow and blue.

13. Put three different simple picture cards on the table. Show him a fourth card that matches one of the three and say, "Give me the one that is the *same as* this one." He will learn what "same" means. Later, prepare the same task, having him choose from four different cards on the table.

14. Give him five small toy dogs and five small toy people. (Some toy companies pack small toys as counting toys, but you will now use them for sorting.) Also have two open boxes on the table. Tell him, "Put the dogs in the dog box and the people in the people box." Show him how to sort them and put them into the boxes; then let him do it by himself.

15. Cut pictures of foods and dogs from magazines. Put two boxes on the table. Give him pictures of five foods and five dogs. Tell him, "Put the things we eat in one box and the dogs in the other box."

16. Let him help you set the table and place the spoons, forks and knives at each place. He will learn to sort the flat-

ware and to place the pieces correctly on each side of the
plate.

Language

The baby is learning many new words these days. He is
probably able to put two or more words together: "All
gone"; "Eat now." He still needs your help in learning new
words. Pictures of objects and actions are good teaching aids.

1. When showing him picture books, ask, "Where is the
dog?" "Where is the apple?" Show him how to point to the
object in the picture.

2. If you point to pictures as you say the names of the
objects, he will eventually repeat the words and begin to
recognize many things in pictures: "Duck," "Apple," "Girl,"
"Lady."

3. Ask him to show you how to *use* certain objects in
pictures. For example, show him a picture of a cup and say,
"Show me what you do with this." If he does not pretend to
drink, show him by pretending you are holding a cup in your
hand and drinking.

4. Play a game of taking turns asking and naming pictures. Point to a picture and ask him to name it; then give
him a turn to ask you to name what he points to.

5. Hand and finger puppets are good to use in telling
stories and acting them out. Give him a chance to imitate
what you do.

6. Give him a toy telephone to use for pretend conversations. He will enjoy imitating your speech.

7. Continue teaching him the names of objects he does
not always see around the home. ("This is a screwdriver.")
Then ask him to find it among other things: "See, all of
Daddy's tools. Where is the screwdriver?"

8. Ask him to name the object: "What do you call this?"
as you point to the screwdriver. He may not remember. Tell
him and see if he can say it.

9. Teach him action words when he does something or sees action in pictures. For example, when he throws a ball, say, "Johnny throws the ball," or "Mommy throws the ball," etc. When he sees a picture of boys playing ball, say, "The boy throws the ball." Show him pictures of familiar actions— eating, running, mother cooking, father hammering.

10. During this period he will begin to use pronouns: I, me, you, he. At first he will get them mixed up. He may say, "Me want" instead of "I want," or "Mommy, help you" when he means "Mommy, help me." Most adults do not use pronouns when talking to a child but if you use them yourself, he will learn to use them properly. Mother should say, "*I* will do it," but she tends to say "*Mommy* will do it." Use *I* and not *Mommy* or *Daddy* when speaking about yourself. If he makes a mistake with his pronouns, do not correct him directly. He will correct himself if you say the proper word, and when you play speech games. We usually do not stop to think about how difficult it is to learn pronouns. The child hears, "*You* do it," but must within his own thinking translate this to mean "*I* should do it."

11. Play the game "This is the way we wash our clothes." Or "eat our lunch," "throw our ball." He can mime action, and will soon learn to say or sing some of the words while you sing the song and go through the actions.

12. Sing and play simple finger games: "Put your finger in the air," "Where is the beehive?" "Where is thumbkin?"

13. Repeat simple nursery rhymes and sing songs to him. He will enjoy the sound and the rhythm, even though he may not understand the meaning. Do not expect him to repeat songs and rhymes or drill him to do so; at this age his speech should be used for telling you things that he understands and wants to communicate to you. You will find that he will say the last word of a line if he hears a rhyme often enough; he will enjoy it without necessarily understanding the meaning.

14. Read a very short and simple story about a little girl or a little boy of his own age. He will associate himself with the story: "I eat breakfast too." "I go swimming too." "I have a sweater too."

15. He may now be ready for you to read a longer story to him. Choose a simple story; he may like it read to him over and over and over again. If he should not want to sit still long enough to be read to, continue showing him pictures instead. Bedtime is a good occasion for telling stories; however, one story and then lights out. He should not be able to get you to tell him one story after another to delay his bedtime.

Many of his words are still not understood by anyone except the members of his family. When he is first learning to make sounds and put them together to make words he will, of course, sometimes say them incorrectly. Unfortunately parents are sometimes proud of the fact that "no one can do things for my baby but me." This is, of course, a serious mistake because the child must eventually play with other children, communicate with a baby sitter, and go to school. He needs to learn to get along with others when still a baby —it becomes more difficult to teach him to adapt to and communicate with others as he gets older.

No child is going to learn to talk if he does not want to. Parents cannot make him talk; they must create in him the desire to talk. When parents learn the meaning of the child's gibberish and gestures, they learn *his* language, but he does not learn theirs. If he forgets a word, simply supply it for him and he will use it again. In general, however, simply show him that you do not understand what he wants when he uses grunts and gestures. Even if you do understand, pretend, as a way of training him, that you do not. If you do not get angry but simply show him that he is not understood, he will be motivated to talk and make himself understood.

Help the baby correct his *own* baby talk. This, too, he

must *want* to do. Three things will help. First: Speak properly yourself; do not use his baby words because you think they are cute. Second: Do not be afraid to *think* that he needs correction. A baby word for a real word is useful only until he is able to say the real word. Third: Do *not* correct him while he is talking and do not tell him that he is wrong. Criticism is always discouraging, making us feel that we cannot ever do well. This is true for babies too. Remember, you cannot make him or force him to do anything nor can *you* correct his speech even if you try. Instead, he must be encouraged to speak well and to feel able to correct himself.

16. Keep a list of the words that need improvement and then use these yourself in talking to him. Do not call attention to them, but simply say each one rather slowly and more carefully than usual. You might talk to yourself as you prepare a meal if he is within hearing distance: "I like eggs for breakpast—oh, not break*p*ast, break*f*ast, *ffffff*, break*f*ast"; or, "I think I'll cook *p*asgetti; no, not *p*asgetti, *sp*aghetti, *spa, spa,* spaghetti." Do not look at him so that he thinks you are talking to him; just talk to yourself, showing him that people correct themselves. He may enjoy what you are saying and think it great fun. He will want to speak well and will be motivated to correct himself if he does not fight his parents about this.

17. Play games in which you say a word incorrectly and he corrects you. Use words that he used to mispronounce but now says correctly. For example, Mother say, "Itto." Child corrects her and says, "No, little." Mother says it correctly. Mother says, "Shobel." Child says, "Shovel." Mother repeats it correctly, etc.

18. If he does not say all the parts of a word, clap hands with each syllable as you say the word: "breakfast" (two claps) It is fun to do this with names: "John-ny Jones" (three claps)

19. Children sometimes do not hear the beginning sounds of words. A child may hear "Mile" when you say "Smile," or "Itto" when you say "Little." Rhyming can help him hear beginnings of words and it is fun: "Daddy, waddy, paddy, kaddy," or "Chickie-wickie" or "Clockie-wockie," or "Little, dittle, mittle." (He may say, "Litto, ditto, mitto" for the latter; this is all right if you are working on *beginnings* of words—you cannot work on both endings and beginnings of words at the same time.

20. Give him examples of words with different endings. He will like "Fee, fi, fo, fum" or "Too, toe, tie, tee."

21. He may make a pun and laugh. Encourage this by repeating what he thinks sounds funny and enjoy it with him. If you can make a pun when you play, laugh and he will enjoy it and say it too. Puns are the beginning of humor.

22. Show him how words can be taken apart and put together again, so that he can better hear the beginnings and endings of words. It is hard to hear the start of words beginning with *s, l, a,* because they are sounded softly. Take words apart that he says correctly: "Mom-my." Make it a game; then you can do this with a word that he says incorrectly: "A-way."

NOTE: Remember, do not interrupt his conversation when he is speaking incorrectly. It is most important that the child *correct himself,* and this is best accomplished by word games introduced during game time. The child who is severely corrected when he is trying to communicate may be so discouraged that he develops speech problems such as stuttering. He may become tense and hesitant because he feels he is not good enough at speech; or he may become angry and assert his own power by continuing to speak incorrectly.

SAMPLE DAILY ACTIVITY PROGRAMS—Twenty-one to Twenty-nine Months

The following sample activity programs are only suggestions to help you plan. Each day you could select the activities for a program so that they include at least one activity from each category of training—fine motor, gross motor, problem solving, language, etc. Determine which activities you will use in your structured educational play period and keep equipment and toys separate from his others so that they remain fresh and exciting to him. As the activities become more difficult, your baby may not wish to participate in some. You should devote only a short time to such activities, presenting them at the beginning of his structured play. Explain that he may do something you know he likes to do when he finishes the activity he may not enjoy so much. For example, if he does not like to count pennies, you might tell him to count them only once, and then he can play with play dough or blow bubbles (if he really likes these). He will probably enjoy counting when it becomes easier for him.

Activities are listed briefly *in these examples of how you might put together a daily activity program for your baby. These same activities are often described in greater detail on the preceding pages, and there you will find, under the following categories, many more activities to choose from to give your baby's daily program variety and interest.*
Fine Motor Activity, page 169
Gross Motor Activity, page 171

Daily Program I

FINE MOTOR ACTIVITY
√ Turn switches on and off
√ Jigsaw puzzle

GROSS MOTOR ACTIVITY
√ Run and climb
√ Play ball

SMELLING ACTIVITY
√ Let him smell contents of jars

SELF-AWARENESS
√ Draw an outline of his hand

IMAGINATION
√ Allow him time to make up his own play

TIME
√ "Time for ——"

WEIGHT
√ Let him hold heavy and light objects

SELF-CARE
√ Dressing lessons

PROBLEM SOLVING
√ Graduated rings

√ Match "big" and "little"

LANGUAGE
√ Point to pictures in book
√ Name objects found in pictures
√ Pretend to use object in picture

Daily Program II

FINE MOTOR ACTIVITY
√ String beads

GROSS MOTOR ACTIVITY
√ Play "hide and seek"
√ Play outdoors

SELF-AWARENESS
√ Draw outline of his foot

IMAGINATION
√ Doll play

TIME
√ "Before" and "after"
√ "Yesterday" and "today"

SELF-CARE
√ Washing lesson

PROBLEM SOLVING
√ "Give me the big one"
√ Jigsaw puzzle

LANGUAGE
√ Pretend phone conversations
√ Teach names of objects
√ Help him use pronouns

Daily Program III

FINE MOTOR ACTIVITY
√ Pegboard

GROSS MOTOR ACTIVITY
√ Play "hide and seek"
√ Play with wagon

SELF-AWARENESS
√ Draw an outline of his body

IMAGINATION
√ Let him pretend

TIME
√ "First" and "last"
√ "Today" and "tomorrow"

SELF-CARE
√ Tooth-brushing lesson

PROBLEM SOLVING
√ Nested cups
√ Form box
√ "One" and "Many

LANGUAGE
√ Action words
√ Finger games
√ Game of correcting mother

Daily Program IV

FINE MOTOR ACTIVITY
√ String beads
√ Screws and screwdriver

GROSS MOTOR ACTIVITY
√ Walk on tiptoe

SELF-AWARENESS
√ Felt doll on flannel board

TIME
√ Future tense

WEIGHT
√ Small boxes containing light and heavy objects

SELF-CARE
√ Dressing lesson

PROBLEM SOLVING
√ Name "big" and "little" circle
√ Chip or button design

LANGUAGE
√ Read story about child his age
√ Clap hands along with pronouncing syllables of words

Daily Program V

FINE MOTOR ACTIVITY
√ String beads
√ Jigsaw puzzle

GROSS MOTOR ACTIVITY
√ Somersault
√ Try to stand on one foot

SMELLING ACTIVITY
√ Smell contents of various jars

SELF-AWARENESS
√ Jigsaw puzzle of human figure

TIME
√ "Slow" and "fast"

SELF-CARE
√ Washing lesson

PROBLEM SOLVING
√ "One for me and one for you"
√ Match colors
√ "Give me the red"

LANGUAGE
√ Game taking turns asking names of pictures
√ Rhyming words

Daily Program VI

FINE MOTOR ACTIVITY
√ Draw with crayons

GROSS MOTOR ACTIVITY
√ Play "ring around the rosie"
√ Play ball

SELF-AWARENESS
√ Human figure made of play dough

TIME
√ Past tense

SELF-CARE
√ Tooth-brushing lesson

PROBLEM SOLVING
√ "Big" and "little"
√ Chip or button design
√ Sort pictures

LANGUAGE
√ Change endings of words
√ Take words apart and put them together

Activity Programs

RUNNING, CLIMBING, TALKING

THE NATURAL play of children offers many learning situations in which the child explores his environment and masters the movement of his muscles. For the most part, the child learns through the experiences that happen to him every day when moving around in the home. The activities of the previous chapters were designed to teach your child to learn, in addition, by using all his senses. If you have helped him build good work habits, he should now be able to sit still for longer periods of time and work with interest and courage to try to solve difficult tasks. He should feel that he himself is in control of his learning, and that learning new things is exciting. He should feel that the importance of learning is for himself and not for his parents or teachers. Strange as this may seem, many children in schools today neither care nor feel a need to learn. They think they go to school only because they are supposed to go to school. Such an attitude reveals the child's lack of responsibility toward his own well-being and possibly his discouragement about life in general, even at such a young age. It is unfortunate that many children entering kindergarten or first grade are ill-prepared to adjust to the social situation in school and to do the work. Each child comes to school having had very different experiences within the first few years of life; each has developed his own style of understanding things he sees, hears and touches. The teacher, however, faced with many different children at the same time, usually teaches everyone in the same way. Thus many of these children feel lost—they do not understand the work or even pay attention to what is going on. They soon give up in extreme discouragement; they daydream or misbehave in some other way.

The child must be encouraged to feel that learning is exciting, an essential part of living, and meaningful to him and his interests. Engaging in educational play activities at a very young age will help the child to achieve this attitude. By working with problems and their solutions, he can test himself and begin to build inner discipline as well as self-confidence. He learns to complete tasks for the feeling of satisfaction he gets from his own efforts. After a child has learned to work this way in play situations, he is able to tackle school learning quite easily. He does not fight learning as something more important to his parents than to himself; he will be able to go on to more difficult learning as he gets older.

By now, in the child's third year of life, his language and thought processes develop by leaps and bounds. Therefore this section deals with more activities involving language and concepts than do the previous sections. Using the activities that follow, as well as those of the past chapters, will prepare him for entering nursery school at age three or four, as well as kindergarten at age five. He must have encouragement from you in order to keep trying when he finds things hard to do. The child looks to adults for encouragement, and if he does not receive it he loses his ambition.

CHAPTER XII | ACTIVITY PROGRAMS—
THIRTY TO
THIRTY-SIX MONTHS

THE YOUNGSTER of about two and one-half to three years old is now much more a child than an infant. He walks, runs, climbs, and tries language and social skills. He still has a long way to go in his speech, although he can say many things and understand many more. He is learning language readily now. He needs practice in learning to be adaptable, both at home and in a play group. At this age children often become ritualistic, insisting that daily routines and activities be followed to the letter. For example, he may think that eating *must* include a certain plate at a specific place on his table, and certain foods at a certain time of the day. Or, bedtime must include a precise routine of a bath, a drink, a story, a trip to the bathroom, a good-night kiss for and from everyone, tucking in; only then can lights be turned out for sleep. These rituals are his way of showing that he has learned about the way things are done in his family. However, he may also be indicating, "You must do it exactly *my* way."

Many older books on child rearing suggest that a child of this age "needs" to be difficult and should be given his own way from the time he is about two and a half until three years of age or he will be unhappy. These books then say that at age three he will become more cooperative. However, we are finding more and more mothers who say, "I know that the books say that he will be difficult to handle when he is two and a half, but he is now way past three and he *still* wants his own way all the time, and expects us to do as he says!"

Parents are asking for trouble when they accept the idea that the two-and-a-half-year-old "needs" to be given his own way and that at three he will no longer "need" his own way. Any time a child is given his own way, he continues to expect it. It is not necessary to agree with him. If you suit your actions to your words, he will understand very quickly that the family will not put up with his tyrant's tactics, and he will thus get along much better for the rest of his life. Under no circumstances does a child at any age "need" to be given his own way. He can learn very early that parents too have rights, and that mutual respect is a necessary part of family and community life.

At times when the child is difficult, humor will go a long way. It is never wise to laugh *at* a child, but when situations get tense, seeing the funny side will help avoid your taking it too seriously and getting upset, and will often calm down the child as well. Humor is a safeguard against undue tensions and anger.

When parents adopt a kind but firm attitude, the child will understand what is expected of him; he will know his parents mean what they say and will be willing to cooperate. It is important that the family define *as a group* what are the best rules for getting along well with one another. By age two and a half or three it is entirely possible to include the youngster in a weekly family meeting at which time the fun things that can be done together as well as the best ways of solving problems can be decided. Children who are reared with such democratic procedures are not as rebellious as are those who are reared with parents as "boss." They are treated with respect and, in turn, show far more respect for their parents.*

The following educational play activities are suggested for this age. A daily one-hour structured play period with either parent is recommended. The fine motor, language, and problem-solving activities should be done at the child's table.

Fine Motor Activity

1. Show him how to draw a circle, a square and a triangle; these may take time to teach.

2. Let him paint with finger paints and water colors.

3. He can make designs by pasting bits of paper and cloths of various colors on a sheet of paper. This is called collage.

* A good book from which you may learn democratic ways of child-rearing is *Children: the Challenge*, Dreikurs, R., and Soltz, Vicki. New York: Hawthorn Books, Inc., 1964.

Papers describing Family Council are available from the Oregon Society of Individual Psychology, Newsletter, M. Bullard, Editor. 1320 NW 13th St., Corvallis, Oregon 97330.

4. Pictures made by connecting dots are fun. Draw a picture outlined by dots and have him connect the dots with a pencil.

5. Show him how to cut with scissors.

6. Let him practice lacing shoes. A toy shoe frame or large shoe would be easier for practice than his own shoe.

7. Sing and play nursery rhymes and finger games.

Gross Motor Activity

1. He will enjoy using climbing equipment both indoor and out.

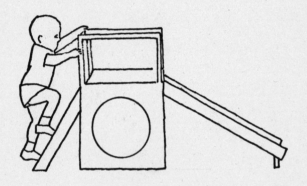

2. Crawling through a tunnel or small space is fun and teaches him the measure of space he occupies. A tunnel may be purchased or several large boxes or crates may be used to make one.

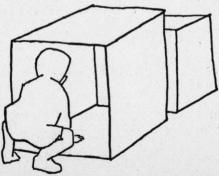

3. He will enjoy slides and swings.

4. He will now be able to learn to ride a tricycle.

5. Play ball with larger and smaller balls. Have him kick the ball as well as throw it.

6. Show him how to walk and run to the rhythm of music or drum beat.

Self-awareness

1. Let him draw a circle with a pencil, crayon, paintbrush or felt pen. Show him how to draw eyes, nose and mouth on the "face."

2. Draw an incorrect picture of a human figure (arms coming from head instead of shoulders, mouth missing from face) and ask him, "What is wrong with the picture?"

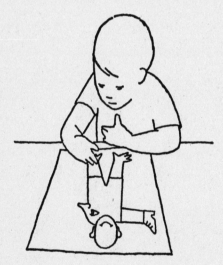

3. Sing songs stressing parts of the body; you can make these up or find them in collections of children's songs ("Put your finger on your nose, on your nose," "If you're happy and you know it, clap your hands").

4. Show him how to stretch all his muscles while he is on the floor, and then how to relax.

5. While he is on the floor, tell him to move both legs, both arms, one leg, one arm. (His limbs should remain touching the floor while doing the movements.)

6. Stand facing him. Tell him that he should pretend that you are his mirror and that he should do whatever you do (touch head, elbow, knee).

Imagination and Dramatic Play

In their dramatic play young children enact the roles of adult life. They do not create an unreal world; they try to make it clear to themselves what the adult world is all about. Such play is also one way of handling their special problem of being little in a world of big people. When a child has a chance to be the big mother, father, bus driver or repairman he has a chance to feel important and to be big for a while.

Toys are most enjoyable when the child can imagine and pretend with them. He will pretend that a doll or even a bundle of rags is a real baby. A broomstick or an old broken chair can be a horse. A large box can be a tent, cave or castle. Blocks can be a train, boat, kitchen or jail. Imagination has led to all the great developments of civilization. It is important to encourage your child's imaginative development. The aim of teaching should not be merely to make him understand things or to memorize facts, but to touch his imagination, to stimulate in him, deep down inside, the will to learn and create new things from what he knows and learns. Maria Montessori, the inspiring educator, stated that the child has an intelligence which "grows under the heat of a flaming imagination."

Toys that inspire the child to imitate the adult world and help him in imaginative play are available in great variety: housekeeping toys, dolls, doll carriage, doll bed, broom, sweeper, toy telephone, animals, dump trucks, milk wagon, fire engine, farm sets, garage and gas station, and the like. It is not necessary to purchase all of these. Young children learn to create by using large blocks, boxes, chairs, old clothes and whatever else they find around the house to use in dramatic play.

Drawing

Drawings made by children have been the object of serious study by child psychologists, who recognize them as a form of expression as important as language. Modern children draw for much the same reasons as did primitive man when he used picture writing to express feelings or ideas. The child first draws to express himself. At first he seems just to scribble. Gradually his drawings become pictures; that is, he knows, and later you too can recognize, what the picture is about. This usually does not happen until he is three or four years old.

Crayons and paper should be given to him by the time he is eighteen months old. The sheets of paper should be large enough to allow free arm movements. The first crayons should also be large—large enough to be grasped by his entire fist; later as finer muscle coordination develops (at about four years) smaller crayons that may be controlled by the thumb and forefinger can be used.

Many children have been discouraged in their efforts to draw by the criticism of adults who think the child's drawing is an attempt to make an actual work of art rather than his form of self-expression. The enjoyment that a youngster gets from drawing and his own progress in that task are far more important than the opinion of adults looking at the results.

Time

1. He will be able to tell the difference between "yesterday," "today" and "tomorrow" fairly well.

2. He will use the past tense of verbs more frequently.

3. Explain ahead of time what is going to happen during a period of a few hours. For example, "First we go to school, then we come home to eat lunch, then we have a nap."

4. Ask him to tell you what he has done during a period of time when he has not been with you.

Problem Solving

1. Cut two sets of circles—two large, two medium, and two small—out of cardboard. They should all be the same color so that you do not confuse teaching color with teaching size. Put one set of circles on the table. Give the other circles to him one at a time and say, "Put the little one with the little one." "Put the big one with the big one." "Put the medium one with the medium one."

2. Compare big and little things in the home (pencils, cookies, boxes).

3. Give him three balls, each of a different size, and play a game in which he asks you, "Which one do you want?" You answer either "Big ball," "Little ball," or "Medium ball." He will especially like this game when he stands at the top of a flight of stairs and throws them down to you.

4. Give him three nested boxes to place one into the other. It is best to start with boxes quite different in size so that there is a lot of space between boxes. They are then easier to place. After he can put three boxes together, give him four, then five.

5. Turn the boxes upside down and show him how to build a tower, starting with the largest on the bottom and the smallest on top.

6. Puzzles with as many as ten to fifteen pieces will challenge him and extend his attention span. Give him puzzles that will keep him working but are not so difficult as to be discouraging. You can help him at first, but do not do the puzzle for him. Let him show *you* how to do it.

7. The form box will be easier for him now. He will probably be able to place all of the shapes in the proper holes.

8. Put two boxes on the table and tell him, "Put one penny in this box and one penny in that box." Show him how to place the pennies in the boxes.

9. Put two boxes on the table and show him two pennies held between your fingers. Have him show you "two" also. Tell him, "Put two pennies in this box and two pennies in that box." He probably will not be able to do the task if he puts in one and then you expect him to put in another. He will be able to see "two" as a unit, but will not understand one plus one more.

10. In time you can go up to five pennies in each of five boxes. To make the game more interesting, after he places the pennies you can pretend that each of the boxes holds money for different members of the family and that you are going to buy candy at the store for him, for Mother, sister, etc. Move the pennies to another side of the table and pretend that area is the store and you the storekeeper.

11. Teach him to count to ten. At first he will not know the meaning of the words, but he will learn that those are the words used for counting, and he will like to say them.

12. Show him how to count the fingers on his hand.

13. Ask him, "How old are you?" Show him how to hold up the proper number of fingers.

14. Sing counting songs with him ("Ten Little Indians").

15. When he eats cookies, let him count them first.

16. Let him stack blocks, and then ask him to count them.

17. When he reads a book and there are several animals or objects, ask him, "How many butterflies are there?" Let him count them.

18. Cut numerals 1, 2, 3 out of sandpaper. Tell him the names of the numerals and let him trace his finger over them so that he can not only see the shape but feel it too. He will soon learn their names.

19. Cut letters of the alphabet out of sandpaper or purchase them in the dime store or toy store. Teach him a few at a time. Do not work at this too long.

20. Put a red, a blue, and a yellow cardboard square (two by two inches) on the table. Give him a red one identical to the one on the table and say, "Put this with the one just like it, the *red* one." Do the same for the yellow and the blue.

21. Put the three colored squares on the table and say, "What color is this?" as you point to each one. If he does not know the color, tell him and see if he repeats it.

22. Let him name colors of things found in the home (red dress, blue dress, etc.).

23. On the table, place four pictures, all alike but one. Ask him to give you the one that does not belong with the others. When he gives it to you say, "Yes, it is *different*." Use the word "different" the next time you play the game: "Give me the one that is different."

24. Cut out pictures of foods, dogs, people, cats and birds. Give him ten foods and ten dogs, saying, "Put the things we eat in one box and the dogs in another box."

25. Give him pictures of ten dogs, ten foods, and ten birds. Now he will have three things to sort into the boxes. Use the other pictures at other times.

Language

As the child uses his senses of seeing, hearing, tasting, smelling and feeling, and then learns words about these sensations, he begins to learn and use language. He learns by listening to the speech of other people and by using speech of his own as he plays with objects or looks at pictures. Usually the child absorbs what he senses (just by living at home) without actual lessons. However, in play activities you can help him expand this knowledge.

Poor language development is one of the most frequent reasons for failing in school. Although every child learns to name things, this is not enough to help him get along in school. He must understand and properly use many other words—not only the names of things but also descriptions of things (whether they are big, small, red, white, heavy). He must also understand action words: running, skipping, moving, walking, and the words that describe these actions: fast, slow, quick. He must understand the differences between the many small words of language: in–on; all–some; over–under. With toys and pictures, you can teach these in his play activities.

1. Teach him about the *kinds* of things he sees either in real life or in pictures (this car is *blue;* this car is *red;* this pencil is *big;* this pencil is *little*).

2. Teach him about *how* things move (the car goes *fast;* the turtle moves *slowly;* the airplane flies *high*).

3. Cut action pictures from magazines and coloring books (a child throwing a ball, washing, gardening, ironing) and say, "What is the boy doing?" If he does not know, tell him and ask him again. He will learn the meaning of actions and start to learn to tell a story about a picture. It is best to start with pictures in which he already understands such actions.

4. He must learn the little words—the prepositions we use all the time. Ask him to put the penny *in* the box, *on* the box, *under* the box, *over* the box, *between* your fingers, *under* your shoe, *over* your head.

5. Teach him opposites in play activities or in pictures:

Boy—Girl: brother, sister, pictures of children

Cry—Laugh: dramatic play; looking in mirror

Down—Up: hold ball up or down; book up on shelf, car down on floor; "ring around the rosy (all fall *down*)"

Full—Empty: pour milk in glass (full); after drinking, it is empty

Goodbye—Hello: when you see him come into room say "Hello," or when you come home; when he leaves the room say "Goodbye"

Hard—Soft: Touch things like stone, sponge, board, feather

Hot—Cold: parent's coffee, milk, cocoa, juice, your hands when it is cold outdoors

Large—Small (or Big—Little): balls, cars, truck, boxes, dolls

New—Old: new toy, old toy; new shoes, old shoes; new house (if you move to another home) and old house

Open—Shut (or Open—Close): boxes, picture of refrigerator open or closed

Over—Under: over his head, under his chair; over—under box

Quiet—Loud: rhythm instruments; radio, inside and outside voice when playing (use quiet indoors)

Round—Square: geometric cutouts, form box, cookies

Slow—Fast: walk, run, rhythm instruments, playing with cars and trains

Stop—Go: run and stop; playing with cars

Throw—Catch: playing ball

Walk—Run: start walking and change to running

6. Teach him how to make negative statements by asking him questions. Show him an apple and say: "Is this an orange? No, this is *not* an orange." Tell him to repeat your answer after you ask the question so that he learns what you want him to say. Show him a cup and say, "Is this a spoon?" He should answer, "No, this is *not* a spoon." If he does not make a negative statement, you say it, and then tell him to repeat it.

7. Many objects can be made plural by adding an *s;* one chair, two chairs; show him the objects and tell him to say the plurals. Since these endings are often hard to hear, emphasize them by buzzing at the end of the word (if it is a *z* sound): "chair*zzzz*"; "spoon*zzzz*"; if an *s* sound, hiss the endings: "cup*ssss*."

The child's vocabulary grows fast during this period. At this time he will try to combine words, thus improving his ability to tell you about experiences or ask for what he wants. He used to express an entire idea with one word. When he said "Wah-wah," he meant water, that he wanted some, and that he wanted some right now. He may now speak in simple sentences You can help him combine words.

Some children, after being able to put two or three words together, go back to a rather complicated jargon; in time they then go back to speech. This jargon probably sounds to the child who uses it like the kind of talk he hears around him. Usually such a child has parents who talk a great deal. Many children never revert to this jargon stage. They go from one-word statements to two words, then three, and finally to sentences. Usually parents of such children speak only a few chosen words to them at one time. They are not surrounded with constant—and to them meaningless—chatter, and they usually are ahead in speech development because they are able to hear those words and then say them. They do not have to work at listening to a barrage of words, picking out a word or two that they can understand.

8. Tell him a phrase for what he is doing. "Johnny go out"; "Bath now"; "All gone."

9. Teach him how to use "and." Put two objects on his table and say, "Ball *and* doll"; "Paper *and* pencil."

10. Tell him what the teddy bear does as you make the teddy bear do it. "Teddy eats," "Teddy dresses," "Teddy goes bye-bye."

11. Whenever he can say more than two words in one statement, encourage him to say a whole sentence. For example, if he says, "Johnny water," you say, "Yes, you want water; say, 'I want water.'" Wait for him to say it before giving it to him. If you find that both of you get angry when you tell him how to talk, *stop at once!* It isn't worth a fight. Simply give him the water, and at another time you can pretend that you do not understand what he says.

WARNING: Do not insist that he say something unless you are pretty sure that he has the ability. Listen to him talk as he plays with other children; this may show you what he is able to say. However, if they baby him, he may not use his full speech ability with them either. If you get along well with your child and have fun together without your criticizing or expecting too much of him, he will learn to speak well, even without lessons from you.

12. Do not correct him while he is talking. Make a note of his speech error, and then make a game of saying it the right way in your play period. For example, if he says "ite," when he means "light," play the *l* game with him (#30, page 212) and then have him try to put the "l" sound in front of the word.

13. Help him store up new words. As you are out with him and he sees something that he has not seen before, give him the words for that experience. If you are walking out-doors, and he sees a boy climbing a tree, he probably will want to stay and watch, or perhaps join in. Tell him, "The boy climbs the tree."

14. Review his newest words daily to help him remember them. The more words he remembers, the less frustrated and angry he will feel when he is talking and trying to make himself understood.

15. Use verb tenses correctly yourself, but do *not* correct him. If he says, "I eated that yesterday," you can say, "Yes, I too ate that yesterday." Actually, in making that mistake, he certainly shows that he is learning about the rules of our language—we say "heat-heated"; "need-needed."

16. All children use pronouns incorrectly at first. A child will say "him" when he means "he," or "me" instead of "I." Most adults do not realize that children can learn to use pronouns between age two and three. We often hear a mother say, "give it to *Mommy*," or "*Mommy* will help you do it." This is unnecessary; she should be saying, "Give it to *me*"; "*I* will help you do it." In that way she gives him practice in hearing the pronouns used correctly. When you hear him say it wrong, apply his statement to yourself, not to him; in this way, you can say it right without actually

correcting *him*. If he says "Me want some," you say, 'I want some too." Do *not* tell him to say "I."

17. Teach him to be considerate and give other people a chance to speak. Many children expect a great deal of attention and they get it by talking constantly. Respect him by giving him a turn to speak with adults, such as during the evening meal. But do not allow him to monopolize the conversation. Parents themselves set a poor example when they chatter constantly. Mutual respect goes a long way in teaching many of the good things we want children to learn.

18. Many children act like a "question box," and parents fall for it because they have been told or they have read that they should talk to the child, take time to answer his questions, serve his needs or help him develop his self-expression. Children's questions should be answered when they want to know something, but undue attention or power over adults is given to the child who constantly asks questions. This often can be handled by a short answer followed by the parent's question in turn and a suggestion to do something. For example, the child is starting a series of questions about pencils: "Mommy, what are you doing?" "Sharpening my pencil." "Why, Mommy?" "So that I can make a shopping list." "What for?" "So we can go to the store." "What will you buy?" "Meat, butter, bread and cookies." "Why, Mommy?" This can go on as long as Mother has the strength to answer; the child can easily outlast her. It would be easier if Mother would answer the first question with, "Sharpening my pencil. Here is a big red pencil for you. Could you draw a picture with this red pencil?" He will probably be glad to try the red pencil.

If the questions have already started before you realize that you are well on the way to an everlasting series, you can say quietly and kindly (never in anger), "You know the answer to that," and just stop talking and go about your work.

As was said in the last chapter, children must be motivated to correct themselves in speech. Through games, you
can help the child learn small differences in sounds which
he does not easily hear: *p, b, k, g, f, v, sh, ch, j, r, l,
t, th* (as in "thank" or "thaw"), *th* (as in then, that, there).
These games will be fun even if he does not have difficulty
with them in speech, and they will help him to gain self-
confidence.

19. *p:* Give him a feather or small piece of paper to hold
near his mouth. Show him how to say *puh* and it will make
the feather or paper move. You can also get liquid bubbles
in the dime store and let him say *puh* and make bubbles.

20. *k:* Show him how to put the tip of his tongue down
behind his lower teeth and say *kuh, kuh, kuh, kuh.* Make up
a pretend animal such as "Batman's Pet," or the "pretend
animal found far away" and do what you think that animal
might do. That animal says *kuh, kuh, kuh.*

21. *g:* Have him keep his tongue tip down behind his
lower teeth as in *k* but tell him to say *guh.* Use a different
pretend animal for this sound.

22. *f:* Let him wet the side of his finger and put it across
his chin under his lips. Show him that it is fun to blow, *fffff,*
until his finger feels cold.

23. *v:* Tell him to hold his finger across the top of his lower
lip and sound like a horn on a big boat, *vvvvvv.* Both of you
move around as if you were a big boat.

24. *sh:* Lay a baby doll down to sleep. Say, "Baby sleeps,
sh," and place your finger over your lips. Give him the doll
and let him put it to sleep and say *sh.*

25. *ch:* Stand in back of him and put your hands on his
shoulders. Now you are a choo-choo train. Say *choo-choo-
choo-choo* as you go around the room.

26. *j:* Pretend you are both frogs. Get down on your
haunches (you can put your hands on the floor in front of

you for balance). As you move up and down, say, "Jump, jump, jump." (He may not say the final *p;* that will not matter just now because you are practicing the *j.*)

27. *s:* Pretend you are both teakettles and pour water into yourselves; then pretend you sit on the stove. Take a deep breath and let the steam go *sssssss*. See if he can say *sssssss* as long as you can; then see if you can say it as long as he does.

28. *z:* Pretend that you are both bees flying around the beehive and then fly out to get honey; say *zzzzzzz* as you get the honey.

29. *r:* Get down on all fours and be lions. Say *rrrrrrrr* at each other. Remember, lions roar loud and seem angry.

30. *l:* Show him how to open his mouth and put his tongue behind his upper teeth and say *llllllll*. Say it louder and say it softer; you can say it higher and lower and change the pitch too. Make it seem like a game.

31. *t:* Show him how to open his mouth and put his tongue up and say *t,t,t,t,t.*

32. *th* (as in "thank" or in "thaw"). Show him how to make his tongue feel cool by putting his tongue outside his teeth and blowing on it. Make the sound last long, *thhhhhh.*

33. *th* (as in the "the," "that"): Tell him to keep his tongue in same position as above, but to make it buzz. You can pretend that you are a bee that buzzes that way instead of *zzzz.*

34. After he can say the above sounds quite well, show him how the sounds can be put together: "ko-la"; "ye-*sssss*"; "pi—t." You can make a game of these too. Pretend to drink the cola; pretend to be a motorboat saying *put-put-put*. Make up your own games or let the child make them up.

35. Teach him to plan with words as he solves a problem. For example, when he is putting together a puzzle, you say, and then have him say with you, "We start at the head; turn it around slowly until the piece will fit; put it in," and so forth. After he learns to say it aloud, tell him to whisper it. And, still later tell him to say it to himself. Research studies have shown us that children who can do this are able to learn to do things more quickly and remember for a longer time.

All little children hesitate in talking or repeat sounds at one time or another. If parents become unduly alarmed and tell their child to "slow down," "think first," or in general call attention to errors in speech, they train him to worry about speech. If he does become worried, the situation deteriorates because he is afraid of saying things wrong. He starts to feel ashamed, and then hesitates even more. It is normal for him to hesitate, repeat, or prolong speech sounds when he is excited, in a hurry, or upset—but this does not mean he has a speech problem. Be sure that you do not create a problem by thinking he has one, or calling it "stuttering." If you do not become alarmed, he will most likely outgrow the difficulty as he learns more words and their use. Do not interrupt or criticize him; listen patiently as he corrects himself, and don't worry! You must have confidence in his ability to grow up in speech as well as in other things. The only help you can give him is in games and play activities when he is not thinking about a problem—just having fun and talking.

36. When the child is between two and three years old he can learn the letters of the alphabet, the sounds that they make, and also begin to learn to read a few words. If he has been given the lessons in this book, he will be able to start learning to read at about age three, providing you use a good method for teaching your child to read. I highly recommend the reading lessons in the book *Give Your Child a Superior Mind,* by Siegfried and Theresa Engelmann (Cornerstone Library, New York, 1981)

SAMPLE DAILY ACTIVITY PROGRAMS—Thirty to Thirty-six Months

Determine which of the following suggested activities you will use in your structured educational play period and keep the toys you will be using separate from other toys, so that they will remain fresh and exciting to your child. As always, choose at least one activity from each category of training each day.

Activities are listed briefly in these examples of how you might put together a daily activity program for your baby. These same activities are often described in greater detail on the preceding pages, and there you will find, under the following categories, many more activities to choose from to give your baby's daily program variety and interest.

Fine Motor Activity, page 197
Gross Motor Activity, page 198
Self-awareness, page 199
Imagination and Dramatic Play, page 200
Drawing, page 201
Time, page 201
Problem Solving, page 202
Language, page 205

Daily Program I

FINE MOTOR ACTIVITY
√ Draw a circle
√ Finger paint

GROSS MOTOR ACTIVITY
√ Climbing equipment

SELF-AWARENESS
√ Draw a face

TIME
√ "Yesterday," "today," "tomorrow"

PROBLEM SOLVING
√ Match sizes
√ Nested boxes
√ Jigsaw puzzles

LANGUAGE
√ How things move
√ "In," "on," "under"
√ Action words
√ Say the whole sentence

Daily Program II

FINE MOTOR ACTIVITY
√ Make a collage
√ Cut with scissors

GROSS MOTOR ACTIVITY
√ Crawl through tunnel
√ Play ball with large and small balls

SELF-AWARENESS
√ "What is wrong with the picture?"

TIME
√ Past tense of verbs

PROBLEM SOLVING
√ Throw big, little, or medium-size ball down stairs
√ Build a tower of boxes

√ One penny in each of two boxes

LANGUAGE
√ Teach opposites
√ Action pictures
√ Practice *p* sound

Daily Program III

FINE MOTOR ACTIVITY
√ Make pictures by connecting dots
√ Cut with scissors

GROSS MOTOR ACTIVITY
√ Ride a tricycle
√ Climbing equipment

SELF-AWARENESS
√ Songs naming parts of body

DRAMATIC PLAY
√ Allow time for imaginative play

TIME
√ Explain ahead what will happen

PROBLEM SOLVING
√ Jigsaw puzzles
√ Two pennies in each of two boxes
√ Match colors
√ Sort pictures

LANGUAGE
√ Opposites
√ Negative statements
√ Game to practice saying *k*

Daily Program IV

FINE MOTOR ACTIVITY
√ Practice lacing shoes

√ Draw a square
√ Paint a picture

GROSS MOTOR ACTIVITY
√ Play on slides and swings
√ Walk and run to drumbeats

SELF-AWARENESS
√ Stretch and relax

TIME
√ Tell what he has done while away from you

PROBLEM SOLVING
√ Big and little things found in home
√ Place three pennies in each of three boxes
√ Count to ten
√ How old are you?
√ Name colors

LANGUAGE
√ Plurals
√ Teach him to use "and"
√ Give him new word for new experience
√ Practice *f* sound

Daily Program V
FINE MOTOR ACTIVITY
√ Draw a triangle
√ Draw a picture

GROSS MOTOR ACTIVITY
√ Climb through tunnels
√ Ride tricycle

SELF-AWARENESS
√ Sing songs naming body parts

SELF-CARE
√ Practice dressing and washing lessons of Chapter XI if necessary

PROBLEM SOLVING
√ Four pennies in each of three boxes
√ Count to ten
√ Count fingers
√ Count cookies
√ Name colors

LANGUAGE
√ Opposites
√ Negative statements
√ Action words for teddy bear
√ Action words
√ Practice saying *sh* in game

Daily Program VI

FINE MOTOR ACTIVITY
√ Paint with finger paints
√ Make a collage

GROSS MOTOR ACTIVITY
√ Play on slides and swings
√ Play with balls

SELF-AWARENESS
√ Stretch and relax
√ On floor, move both legs

TIME
√ "Yesterday," "today," "tomorrow"
√ Past tense

PROBLEM SOLVING
√ Big and little things in the house

√ Jigsaw puzzles
√ Sing counting songs
√ Stack blocks and count them
√ Name colors of things in home
√ "Different"

LANGUAGE
√ "Between," "under," "over"
√ Pronouns
√ Review his newest words
√ Practice saying *ch* in game
√ Practice saying *j* in game

CHAPTER XIII | # THE HOUSE OF TOMORROW

WITH KNOWLEDGE increasing at the rapid rate of our super-technological age and with the obvious necessity of producing a civilization that can by its own intellect avoid its own ultimate destruction, there is no wonder that serious but happy "educational play" is replacing "aimless play" as the majority activity of early childhood.

Educators are increasingly concerned with the number of school dropouts coming from both slum and well-to-do areas. These young people are so discouraged by failure to do well in school that they do not take their places as contributing members of society. This is not only a social but a personal loss as well. It is obvious that the emphasis in education should be on the prevention of educational deficiencies rather than the making up for those which later develop.

Research in education and psychology has shown that basic intelligence and the motivation to learn, as well as the child's other attitudes, are formed very early in life. In a review of the effect of early environment on intelligence it was estimated that, "50 percent of intellectual development takes place between conception and age four, about 30 percent between ages four and eight, and about 25 percent between ages eight and seventeen." (Benjamin S. Bloom, Stability and Change in Human Characteristics. New York: Wiley, 1964.) What makes the earliest years the most powerful learn-

ing years? Obviously the child is more in control of his circumstances than he is in his school years. He is doing his
own learning through living in the home environment and
through his very own interpretations of that environment
and what happens to him. He is also doing his own learning
through manipulating and experimenting without fear of
failure; because it is fun, he repeats a task over and over
again until he has mastered it. We can no longer afford not
to take advantage of the earliest years of the child to con-
sciously promote a style of life that includes the motivation
to acquire knowledge and the creative ability to use the
knowledge toward a contribution to the culture in which the
child develops and to the world as a whole.

Bringing up children is a difficult and complex task, re-
quiring both order and flexibility. Parents experience many
moments of faint-heartedness and fear of failure in this effort,
in which it is so important to them to succeed. A little systematic planning can be done to make it possible to work
and play together for the satisfaction of the entire family.
We should live *with* our children and not *for* them; we
should make changes in our way of life not primarily
because it is best for the children but because it is best for
the whole family. We should be prepared to know not only
what we must be cautious about and what to avoid, but what
we may expect and welcome. A congenial group, democrat-
ically led, with an outlook of optimism and a readiness to
enjoy the little happenings along the way, will discover together and be stimulated into worthwhile play and work.

Starting with the simple play of infancy, educational activities exist in abundance if the parent will make thought-
ful selections of play materials and will allow the child as well
as herself to create new uses and ideas with things on hand.
The parent can always find a means of amusing while teaching her child, if she cooperates with him in his play. This

play must be wholehearted or the child will lose interest.

Education must not only include the acquisition of facts but the sensitivity to understand others by identifying with them as if being in their skin, seeing with their eyes, and hearing with their ears. Expressing his deep concern for the basic need of man—the need to belong and to face life with courage —Alfred Adler, the world-famous Viennese psychiatrist, wrote in his book, *The Science of Living,* "Only a person who is courageous, self-confident and at home in the world can benefit both by the difficulties and by the advantages of life. He is never afraid. He knows that there are difficulties but he knows that he can overcome them."

Education must include the teaching of courage to face and solve the major tasks of life: getting along with others in the community; making a contribution to society through work; adjusting to love and marriage; being satisfied with one's own self; and being able to see oneself as one individual among a large number of others in the past and future as well as the present playing a part in a great cosmic process. Being able to solve these life tasks will lead the individual to become independent and mature, and to thoughtfully direct his own life.

A Syrian poet tells us what our attitude toward raising children should be:

And a woman who held a babe against her bosom said, Speak to us of Children.
And he said:
Your children are not your children.
They are the sons and daughters of Life's longing for itself.
They come through you but not from you.
And though they are with you they belong not to you.

You may give them your love but not your thoughts,
For they have their own thoughts.
You may house their bodies but not their souls,
For their souls dwell in the house of tomorrow, which you cannot
visit, not even in your dreams.
You may strive to be like them, but seek not to make them like
you.
For life goes not backward nor tarries with yesterday.

You are the bows from which your children
as living arrows are sent forth.
The Archer sees the mark upon the path of the infinite,
and He bends you with His might
that His arrows may go swift and far.
Let your bending in the Archer's hand be for gladness.
For even as He loves the arrow that flies, so He
loves also the bow that is stable.

KAHLIL GIBRAN, *The Prophet* (1923)